C-Rations
FOR THE
WARRIOR'S HEART

3I MEALS FOR THE
LONG MARCH

ROBERT BOARDMAN

ACW
PRESS

ACW Press
Eugene, Oregon 97405

C-Rations for the Warrior's Heart
Copyright ©2003 Robert Boardman
All rights reserved

Cover Design by Alpha Advertising
Interior design by Pine Hill Graphics

Packaged by ACW Press
85334 Lorane Hwy
Eugene, Oregon 97405
www.acwpress.com
The views expressed or implied in this work do not necessarily reflect those of ACW Press. Ultimate design, content, and editorial accuracy of this work is the responsibility of the author(s).

Publisher's Cataloging-in-Publication Data
(Provided by Cassidy Cataloguing Services, Inc.)

Boardman, Robert.

   C-rations for the warrior's heart : 31 meals for the long march / Robert Boardman. -- 1st ed. -- Eugene, OR : ACW Press, 2003.

     p. ; cm.

     ISBN: 1-932124-15-2 — Trade Paper Edition
     ISBN: 1-932124-18-7 — Hardcover Edition

     1. World War, 1939-1945--Personal narratives, American.
2. War--Religious aspects. 3. Courage--Religious aspects.
4. Spirituality. 5. Soldiers' writings, American. I. Title.

D811.A2 B63 2003

940.53/08--dc22   0309

Printed in the United States of America.

⋆ Dedication ⋆

To a literal army of warriors—past and present, non-military and military—who have backed, encouraged, nurtured, prayed for, communicated with and sent Jean and me on our task at home and abroad.

This invisible army is like a Marine tank company maintenance platoon—well back of the front lines, doing their non-glorious, dirty job to keep the steel monsters running, receiving little or no credit or thanks for hard-fought victories. Yet they are absolutely vital to everyday operations and victory on the field of battle.

These unsung friends completely concur with us that victories are won on the battlefield primarily because of the preparation, dedication and exercise of the strength of the inner heart—and not because of superior numbers, equipment and technology.

To this end they have dedicated themselves with Jean and me. They hail from Japan, Korea, Okinawa, Australia and the United States, and are determined with us to keep moving steadfastly toward nourishing a strong, dedicated heart and spirit.

It is impossible to list the names of this army here. We know who they are and we are eternally grateful for each one. They know who they are. "Thank you" seems so utterly inadequate.

Young men have the illusion that death is very remote, an illusion that is normally lost, slowly, by installments, over the years. But war is so extreme, its carnage so agonizing. This illusion is lost all at once and one is driven to the precipice of an intense and sober contemplation on the meaning and significance of life. This powerful effect of war marks a man. The effect that Bob Boardman's book has had on me, through the poignant stories of his own battle experiences and those of others is profound. But unlike other books on war, Bob doesn't just leave you on that precipice, but gives a message of hope based on the most important truth of all.

—First Sergeant David Bishop, US Marine Corps (Ret)

⋆ **Contents** ⋆

✳ **Foreword** ✳

Men discover their true character in the crucible of combat. Few other events in life test the physical, mental, and moral fiber of an individual. The strength of our spirit, of our beliefs, comes through in the most horrific moments of war. This strength is forged by our faith, family, friends, freedom and flag. These are our most precious possessions. They build in men an iron code that enables them, when under fire, to do extraordinary things at the most desperate times.

This book is about men who have faced that moment that tested their spirit and how they rose above their fears to meet the challenge. From these stories of courage we can better understand what it takes to be a hero and how a strong faith can give men the power needed, not only to survive, but also to prevail.

Bob Boardman has given us another labor of love in *C-Rations for the Warrior's Heart*. Like his previous work, *Unforgettable Men in*

Unforgettable Times, it is a book that helps us understand what gives a hero his bravery. It is also a work designed to provide a guide for life's toughest moments with words to comfort, encourage, and counsel.

Semper Fi,
Anthony C. Zinni
General USMC (Ret)

General Anthony C. Zinni,
USMC (Ret)

Robert Boardman USMCR, U.S. Naval Hospital, Philadelphia, December, 1946.

✶ Introduction ✶

We who served in the military have a very good idea of what the word *hero* means. The root comes from the Greek word, *heros*, meaning "protector." Therefore, in these war stories you will read personal accounts about and by men from different branches of the Armed Forces who put their lives on the line. They were *heroes* or *protectors* in every sense of the word. Almost to a man, this inner strength came from their deeply held faith.

Some of the chapters come from the author's writings in his column, *The Chaplain's Corner,* in veteran's publications such as the Marine Corps Tanker's Association magazine. Bob Boardman has written dozens of these reality messages over the years.

One example is "Bud Brenkert's Most Heroic Act." These stories provide the reader with object lessons on how God rules and overrules in our lives in times of combat and stress. They also reveal the tremendous price that was paid for the freedoms we enjoy today.

The other part of Boardman's anthology is a series of war stories, some written by him and some by the men themselves. They write from the heart telling of their wartime experiences. Here is a brief review of a couple of these narratives.

"Open Secrets of Leadership" is about Army Captain Paul Stanley's fighting spirit in the face of the enemy as a Rifle Company Commander, September 1967, in Vietnam. Captain Stanley, a West Pointer, was true to his Corps motto, "Duty, Honor and Country." Speaking from my own personal war experiences, it took guts and faith on the part of Stanley. Flying in the relative safety of his helicopter and seeing his people in trouble, he makes the decision to land under fire. Once on the deck, he drags his wounded men to the chopper for evacuation. Then without hesitation, Captain Stanley turns and leads elements of his unit in a counterattack, driving the Viet Cong from the field. His courage above and beyond the call of duty earned him a Silver Star.

"The Surgeon Who Did Not Want the Medal of Honor" is an eye-catching title with heroic action. On 27 August 1967, Lieutenant Commander David Taft, USN Medical Corps, was awarded the Navy Cross for coolly amputating a Marine's leg embedded with a live rocket in the knee joint. At any moment, this deadly, unstable rocket round could have exploded, killing the patient, the corpsman in attendance, and Dr. Taft. The postscript to this story is a nail biter but I will leave that for you to read. His story contains all the suspense-filled ingredients worthy of a movie drama. The difference is that Dr. Taft's heroic actions were not figments of some movie script writer's prolific imagination.

Bob Boardman became a true believer while serving his country during World War II. He was a "born again Christian" long before it became a familiar term. His spiritual transformation took place in 1943, during the early days of his overseas experience in the First Marine Division. He tells this story in the chapter, "I Was a Dog-Tag Christian." I can verify that Bob Boardman is a true hero in every sense of the word. He put his life on the line in the Marines and served his faith in every clime and place. There is no doubt that this book was inspired by the Lord, using Boardman as the catalyst. My prayer is that its inspirational message will reach into the hearts of men, women and young people throughout our great nation and even beyond our shores.

Enjoy the read . . . each of these stories is truly C-rations for the heart. They clearly reveal that a key element in winning wars resides inside the spirit of man.

Semper Fidelis,
Walter Moore,
Colonel USMC (Ret)

⋆ 31 Meals for the Long March ⋆
Author's Preface

After spending over two years in the Pacific in the famed First Marine Division in World War II, I can attest to the truth of the adage attributed to Napoleon, "An army marches on its stomach." Sometimes our travel was slow, lean and mean, but our chow was the number one concern. Tacitus, the Roman general said:

> *What makes the general's task so difficult is the necessity of feeding so many men and animals. If he allows himself to be guided by the supply officers, he will never move and his expedition will fail.*

Nobody could outdo Marines at scrounging, and chow in any form was often the target of our "requisitioning" skill. In pre-combat preparation and in combat areas, C-rations were the principle staple that fed that monstrous stomach—at least of the land forces. Without controversy the Navy had the best chow with plenty of room aboard ship to stow it. No C-rations for those lads!

C stood for can. Cans of food were issued to individual soldiers and Marines to be carried in their pack or in their tank to eat on the move when there was no field kitchen available. Many a time in combat, I remember, we subsisted on two small cans a day when supplies were short.

In the Korean War in the early 1950s, C- and K-rations were the staple, also. A few years later in Vietnam, C-rations became "Meal, Combat, Individual." After that and before Operation Desert Storm came "Meals Ready to Eat" (MRE) which are still used today.

C-rations during WWII usually came in two metal cans per meal: one heavy and one light. The heavy can held a condensed stew of various kinds and flavors like vegetable stew with meat, pork and beans, ham and eggs, beans and wieners, etc.

The light can contained biscuits, crackers, packets of drink mix like lemon or cocoa powder and instant coffee, sugar, three cigarettes and toilet paper. Oh yes, there was also a bitter chocolate bar, a great source of quick energy. The chocolate was so hard that if carried in the shirt pocket it could save lives by stopping enemy shrapnel! How's that for an environmentally friendly flak jacket?

C-rations

The title of this series of stories, *C-Rations for the Warrior's Heart,* conveys the concept that there is more to fueling a fighting man's strength than physical food. He also needs C-rations for the inner man, the invisible seat of our whole being, the heart, which drives and motivates the body and the mind.

Here is an illustration that may be helpful to show the tripartite being of our nature:

THE WARRIOR–A TRIPARTITE BEING

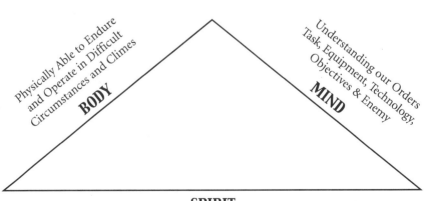

The spirit responds, processes and puts into action the following qualities under the duress of training, serving and warfare:

- Sacrifice
- Loyalty
- Duty
- Respect
- Selfless Service
- Honor
- Fear and Worship of God
- Honesty

- Moral Will
- Integrity
- Personal Courage
- Commitment
- Fairness
- Faith
- Justice
- Forgiveness

and many other qualities

I look upon the spiritual life of the soldier as even more important than his physical equipment. The soldier's heart, the soldier's spirit, the soldier's soul are everything. Unless the soldier's soul sustains him, he cannot be relied upon and will fail himself and his country in the end.

—General George C. Marshall, USA,
Chief of Staff and former Secretary of State

These men about whom I have written are outstanding warriors in their respective battles. It is my great privilege here to either write their stories or to include their own narrative. Many have been decorated for their heroic part in their respective engagements. For the most part their citations have never before been published for the general public, but have gathered dust in some obscure file.

For those who did not receive a citation, I love the words that describe the personally undecorated members of the elite Marine Third Reconnaissance Battalion in Vietnam: *"An even greater number were better honored by the respect of their peers."* See chapters 3 and 6 regarding the Third Recon and members Frank Reasoner and T. Udell Meyers.

The qualities revealed in the lives of every one of the warriors in this book illustrate that most of them, as young men, have learned and partaken of C-Rations for the Heart—which include the intangibles I have listed above under the Spirit of Man. General John A. Lejeune, Eleventh Commandant of the Marine Corps, recognized the centrality of the spirit in man's makeup:

There is no substitute for the spiritual in war. Miracles must be wrought if victories are to be won, and to work miracles men's hearts must needs be alive with self-sacrificing love for each other, for their units, for their division, and for their country.
— Gen. Lejeune, *The Reminiscences of a Marine*, 1929

General Montgomery confirms this salient point regarding the all-important heart and spirit of the warrior:

I have always held the view that an army is not merely a collection of individuals, with so many tanks, guns, machine-guns, etc., and that the strength of the army is not just the total of all these things added together. The real strength of an army is and must be, far greater than the sum total of its parts; that extra strength is provided by morale, fighting spirit, mutual confidence between the leaders and the led and especially with the high command, the quality of comradeship and many other intangible spiritual qualities.
— Field Marshall Viscount Montgomery of Alamein, in his memoirs, 1958

The fighting men in this book represent the Army, Navy, former Army Air Corps, Air Force and Marine Corps. The US Coast Guard, I'm sure, had similar stories. I simply did not discover any in my research. My apologies to these brave warriors, a vital part of our US defense.

The greatest number of combat stories are from World War II. This is natural, I'm sure, because that is my era. After WWII there are ten stories about Vietnam, followed by Korea and Desert Storm.

Out of twenty men whose stories are recounted, as nearly as I can tell, fifteen Purple Hearts were awarded for being wounded in action. Two of the men received two Purple Hearts apiece. E. Boyce Clark, in chapter 10 in Korea, was one of these. His second award cost him his left arm. All twenty of these men paid a high price for the freedom and privileges we have today and so often take for granted.

There are 31 chapters. These are the 31 meals for your long march. One suggestion is to read one chapter a day according to the date. That means, read chapter 6 on the sixth of the month, chapter 7 on the seventh, etc.

Perhaps this method wouldn't work on the first reading, but try it on subsequent readings. Hopefully these stories of courage, honor, commitment and faith and the accompanying meditation and prayer will be an example and inspiration for you to follow as a service person or as a civilian.

Another idea is to read the chapters out loud as a family. My wife Jean and I were amazed at the number of families that did this with my last book, *Unforgettable Men in Unforgettable Times.* Teens and even preteens were deeply interested and involved in reading these true action stories.

May myriads of veterans and active service personnel all over the world—men, women and young people from all walks of life— read these stories and gain a great hunger for C-rations for their own heart.

May they pass these lessons on to others that we not forget the strength of will of the heart and spirit that made our people and nation great in the past. May God be merciful to us and grant us eventual victory in this new war we find ourselves in!

✯ **I** ✯

Leadership
in Wartime

In the British Army there are no good units and no bad units—only good and bad officers and NCOs. They make or break the unit. Today we cannot afford anything but the good ones. No man can be given a more honorable task than to lead his fellow countrymen in war.

We the officers and NCOs owe it to the men we command and to our country that we make ourselves fit to lead the best soldiers in the world. This is so that in peace the training we give them is practical, alive and purposeful, and that in war our leadership is wise, resolute and unselfish.

Leaders are made more often than they are born. You all have leadership in you. Develop it by thought, by training and by practice…

— Field Marshal Viscount Slim of Burma, 1949

Captain Paul Stanley,
US Army, 1967

Paul Stanley today in
Colorado Springs,
Colorado.
Navigator staff

One

OPEN SECRETS OF LEADERSHIP

Paul Stanley's Story

by Bob Boardman

Character is the bedrock on which the whole edifice of leadership rests. It is the prime element for which every profession, every corporation, every industry searches in evaluating a member of its organization.

With it, the full worth of an individual can be developed. Without it—particularly in the military profession—failure in peace, disaster in war, or, at best, mediocrity in both will result.

—General Matthew Ridgway, 1966

Army Captain Paul Stanley's life and death venture on the battlefield in the Republic of Vietnam in 1967 began many years previously, even as a preteen growing up in Glenrock, New Jersey. Selfless instant decisions that almost cost him his life and saved the lives of men in his unit were made on the foundation of a God-fearing upbringing. As a result of his heroics against a well-entrenched Viet Cong enemy, he was awarded our nation's third highest combat decoration, the Silver Star.

Paul Stanley felt most fortunate to be the youngest of five boys because his parents were able to learn much about parenting by the time of his arrival. Through his growth process, he carefully observed his older brothers—which ones to follow and which ones not to emulate.

Family values were vital to making right and courageous decisions later in Vietnam on the battlefield when lives were at stake. These values counted, not only in Paul's life, but in those of the men in his company.

Paul also places great value on competitive sports as a vital leadership building block in his personal life:

Athletics played an important role in shaping my initial leadership values. For instance, excellent conditioning and mastering the fundamentals not only characterizes winning football teams, but it is the stuff great military units from squad to company are made of. The power in modeling the values and commitments you want others to embrace and the incalculable impact of a band of men united by a compelling purpose and commitment to help each other succeed are fundamental to great organizations.

Stanley entered West Point in 1959, right out of high school, and played football on their nationally-ranked team. He was also a second team All-American in the grueling sport of lacrosse.

Upon entering West Point I had in my mind to either get serious about a spiritual pursuit or let it drop lower on my list of things to pick up again after graduation. I had made some commitments to respond to Jesus Christ and even prayed that God would send someone who could help me grow. After all, it was important to those I tended to emulate.

God heard my prayer. At the end of the first week of football practice, the All-American quarterback, Joe Caldwell,

*walked over to some of us freshmen
and invited us to an evening Bible
study discussion group he was
leading. Without even hesitating, I
heard myself say, "Yes sir, I would
like to come!" No one else
responded.*

Not only did Stanley study the Bible
in a group setting with other cadets on
a regular basis, but Joe met Paul in the
early morning, one-on-one, to pray and
meditate on the Holy Scriptures.

*When I graduated four years later in 1963, I was a very dif-
ferent person—not just physically, but in every other way. I
was being changed from the inside out. I had become a child
of God by His initiation, Jesus Christ's intervention for me
and my response to Him as my Savior and personal Leader.
Jesus did not just become a part of my life; He took over the
center of my life and began drawing all aspects of my life into
His. For the first time I experienced a wholeness, an integra-
tion of all of life and a power to live a different kind of
life…and I loved it!*

These leadership building-block principles—watching the
example of his dad and brothers; the rough and tumble of competitive athletics; and then a personal life-changing faith in the Living
God—all prepared Stanley for the battlefield crisis in Vietnam years
later.

After West Point, Stanley was commissioned a new second lieutenant and was sent to Fort Benning, Georgia for rigorous airborne
and Ranger training. His first assignment was two and a half years
in Germany, followed by a short stint again at Fort Benning, this
time as an instructor. Then on to Vietnam, where he joined the
Fourth Battalion 199th Infantry Brigade. He soon became commander of Company C.

On 4 September 1967, Captain Stanley was in a helicopter flying a
reconnaissance mission, while units of Company C were conducting

a search and destroy operation on the ground. Captain Stanley suddenly spotted a platoon-sized Viet Cong force moving toward their company flanks, but the flank platoon had not yet seen them. Here is a vivid picture of the action that followed from Stanley's Silver Star citation:

> *Quickly grasping the situation, Captain Stanley directed that a gunship be used to transport a reinforcing squad across a river to the insurgent's location. Surprised by the sudden arrival of the friendly force and its rapid advance, the Viet Cong began to retreat, firing as they moved. When the squad halted to assist a seriously wounded member, the Viet Cong took advantage of the pause to return to a bunker to deliver suppressive fire on the friendly force. Observing the battle from his helicopter, Captain Stanley directed that his aircraft be landed. Courageously disregarding the enemy fire, he leaped from the craft and assisted in placing several wounded soldiers on the helicopter for evacuation. After he had reorganized the squad, he led an attack on the entrenched enemy, completely exposing himself as he fired his weapon and threw hand grenades. His aggressive charge toward the Viet Cong caused them to panic and retreat. Captain Stanley's aggressive actions and personal bravery served as an example for his men to emulate, inspiring them to greater effort. Captain Stanley's extraordinary heroism and dedication to duty were in keeping with the highest traditions of the military service and reflect great credit upon himself, his unit and the United States Army.*
>
> *Authority: By direction of the President under the provisions of the Act of Congress, approved 9 July 1918.*

Paul Stanley's own words sum up the heart of his leadership during the extreme stress of combat:

> *Christ seemed very close to me when I was sent to Vietnam. Despite the pressure of active combat, He was my source of strength. Many of my troops commented on how calm I remained regardless of the circumstances, but it was simply because the Lord was real to me. Often I thought of the verse*

in the Psalms: Though I walk through the valley of the shadow of death, I will fear no evil: for You [God] are with me. — Psalm 23.4

✫　　✫　　✫

SCRIPTURE: *You, Lord, will keep him in perfect peace, whose mind is stayed on You: because he trusts in You. — Isaiah 26.3*

PRAYER: *Lord God, when Your enemies appear before me, teach me to fight with Your weapons and be clothed with Your armor—and grant to me Your supernatural peace of heart. Amen.*

LtCol. Walter Moore with Gen. Victor "Brute" Krulak, USMC, Vietnam, 1966

Walter Moore today, at home in Oceanside, California.

Two

WALTER "MUMU" MOORE, MARINE EXTRAORDINAIRE

*It is a notable fact that few men ever leave the Marine Corps
without a feeling of undying loyalty toward it.*
— General Alexander A. Vandegrift, 6 May 1946

R. Boardman's Introduction: Few can ever forget Colonel Walt
Moore. His fellow Marines called him "MuMu," the native word for
filarisis, a tropical malady he acquired early in WWII. This moniker,
which he'd love to shed, has stuck with him to this day. "MuMu"
Moore is a veteran of three wars, experiencing combat in WWII,
Korea and Vietnam. In the course of serving his country, this old
Marine has garnered his share of medals for valor, wounds, meri-
torious service in some strange climes and places. Several foreign

countries, including Spain and the Dominican Republic honored him for extraordinary service. Here are his words:

"I experienced a fair share of close calls in my lifetime, including several attempts on my life during my service as a military advisor while in the Corps. After my retirement and a stint in academia, I returned to the fray in Latin America as a Government "consultant." Still working on the edge…so to speak. Many a time I've wondered why I survived when so many of my comrades paid the supreme sacrifice."

I met "MuMu" Moore on Pavuvu in the Solomon Islands when he first came there and joined C Company, First Tank Battalion after the battle of Peleliu and as we prepared for the battle of Okinawa. He was the Company Executive Officer and I was an enlisted man so we didn't have much contact.

Many years later we met again in 1990 as true followers of the Living God and became as close as blood brothers. Moore retired as a Marine Colonel after thirty-three exciting years. Later in civilian life, Colonel Moore, who is fluent in Spanish, earned a master's and Ph.D. in Latin American History.

Out of many combat stories Walt Moore could have chosen, he selected Operation Colorado/Lien Ket-2 in Quang Tin Province, South Vietnam. The then Lieutenant Colonel Moore commanded the nine-hundred man Second Battalion, Fifth Marine Regiment, First Marine Division. Here is his story:

The second day of the Operation was 7 August 1966, exactly twenty-four years after the famous landing on Guadalcanal by the First Marine Division. I was in a command Huey helicopter returning to my unit from a briefing held at the Brigade & Regimental CP located in Tam Ky. When I left my command earlier, my rifle companies were setting up a perimeter in a deeply wooded assembly area. Once accomplished, the company commanders had orders to send out feeler patrols along several trails. Purpose: to determine the best "back door" approaches to our objective in Hiep Duc Valley. My plan was to depart after dark and quietly move toward this suspected North Vietnam Army (NVA) main force logistics base and attack at first light. Earlier, when Regimental Headquarters ordered me back for the briefings at Tam Ky, I objected to leaving my troops during this crucial period... but to no avail.

It was now about 1500 hours and we were about three-quarters of the way back. I was anxious to get back, so I urged the pilot to speed up. It was a tough order because the terrain looked very much the same. In order to find my battalion position, the plucky pilot dropped the Huey close to the deck as we sped on. Then our troubles started.

We soon flew into an enormous billowing, dry-looking, cottony white cloud. It extended high above us and went right to the ground. The pilot flew by the seat of his pants, feeling his way along, sheets of rain hitting the windshield. If he wasn't disoriented, I sure was. Since I was what was called a "foxhole Christian" and in trouble, I closed my eyes and prayed to God, asking him to show the way. Corporal Henderson, my radio operator, prayed.

Every once in awhile there was a break in the clouds. That wasn't so good either. We were being fired upon. This happened twice as we hurtled along. Tracers shot up, bisecting the sky near enough to force the pilot to change altitude. Time seemed to drag along. Actually, about fifteen minutes had lapsed since we first entered the big cloud. We were tooling along at about one hundred feet. Suddenly as we flew over a flooded area at the edge of a heavy thicket, a couple of signal flares shot up. Yelling into my ear, Henderson, my radio operator, shouted, "There they are!" I yelled back... "Who?" Fighting back at the cockpit noise, Henderson screamed, "The Battalion... The Battalion... Look!" Sure enough it was. As usual, my sharp-eyed right arm was on the ball! As if in agreement, the chopper pilot made a sharp corkscrew right turn, heading down like riding in a fast elevator for a landing site. The pilot told us to jump out as he hovered over the waterlogged field. He dumped the Sergeant Major, Henderson and me in the chest deep water about two hundred yards from the edge of the wooded area. We literally fell into the water as the Huey pulled up and away in a steep climb. He was out of there!

As I wondered why the pilot had hurried, automatic weapons fire started to zip and crack over our heads. I looked toward the friendly side of the tree line and noted some of my men frantically pointing behind me and waving us towards them. It didn't take long to get the message…my Sergeant Major, "Pappy" Henderson and I started doing a crude but frantic breast stroke, bobbing under water, wading… slipping and sliding towards the friendly tree line. Our packs, weapons and gear were hampering our forward movements! The enemy opened up again, with bullets shooting up streams of water as they reverberated alongside. Several Soviet-type RPG rounds thwacked one of the partially submerged burial mounds near us. Too close for comfort!

We, the "frantic three," continued our amphibious trek to safety. In between gulps of dirty paddy water, I kept saying a prayer… "HELP, Lord save us…get us to the tree line…please God." It seemed to take forever to reach safety. The troops were firing over our heads at the enemy on the opposite tree line. Some of the men, with a slightly misguided sense of humor, cheered us on. Finally, a couple of my Marines ran out and pulled us the final few yards to the relative safety of the tree line…we were soaked and muddy…a physical state that was our lot for a long time to come.

Regardless, it felt good to be among my people again. I walked down the trail to a thatch-roofed shack in the middle of a clearing. (For reasons long forgotten, Marines called them "Hoochs.") On the way to the hooch, my men greeted me with irrepressible enthusiasm and cheer. To them, being out in the middle of nowhere was a great but deadly adventure…come what may! I still remember this after all these years.

This native shack served as my Battalion Command Post (CP). For the purposes of mobility and simplicity, my command group was made up of bare essentials only—something the experience of three wars taught me the hard way. On the move I used a tactical command group of about twelve men to control the Battalion's capability to shoot, move and communicate. Also included were the indispensable communicators, our operational life blood. Outside this crowded, leaky, thatch-roofed haven, it was pitch dark, the rain pouring down in sheets. Just as the staff started to brief me on the situation, a real shocker was tossed into our midst!

It was 1930 when the communication officer handed me an urgent message from Regiment. It was cryptic, but telling: "Be advised that a large flight of B-52s (Arc Light Strike) will bomb the vicinity of Hiep Duc Valley at about 0500. Urge you to withdraw from your current location ASAP, etc."

I was shocked to note that the western edge of the map coordinates was about three thousand meters from the forward edge of my leading two rifle companies. I immediately called Regimental Headquarters, telling them it was impossible for me to round up nine hundred men in a rain-soaked jungle anytime soon. The visibility, rain and mud made moving nearly impossible. Most of our tactical radios were out. Thank God that I employed the old WWII jungle technique of light combat wire and sound power phones. My nine hundred or so Marines were counting on me to make the right moves and quickly!

At 2200 with no positive news from the rear, the order went out to all hands to dig "deep holes." What better motivation was available than the threat of this lethal formation of B-52s dropping a carpet of high-explosive bombs on top of us. I called the Company COs and stated our situation. Told them to get their men back down the trail from the edge of the bomb impact area ASAP.

By this time it was about 2400 and no word from Regiment about calling off the Arc Light strike. My worst fears were confirmed: "It was easier said than done!" The Echo Company patrol was still out. If worse came to worse, they could be trapped…somewhere. The patrol leader was a wise combat veteran who knew how to take care of his men. But one B-52 hiccup at 50,000 feet and we would get a load right into our laps.

I was impressed by the collective mood of the Marines around my CP. They were still digging holes and still laughing and joking. Suddenly Chaplain Kane, who was near the command hooch, stood up and began to pray. He asked for God's protective spirit to embrace us. When he finished, I silently repeated the practical words of the "Serenity Prayer."

Then I went into the hooch and got down on my knees and prayed, "God deliver us from this place." I reached into my pack and unraveled the plastic covering of my pocket New Testament. It was a small Gideon International model with the books of Psalms and Proverbs appended. Up to now I had not used it much. All of a sudden, a small voice in my head said, "Walter, why are you still practicing the art of the foxhole Christian? Shutting the Lord out…turning to Him only when in need?" I quickly pushed this self-evident truth out of my mind. The pages were wet and stuck shut. I turned to Psalm 31. The top of the page was titled: *A Prayer for Help!* Suddenly my eyes fell upon verses 3, 4 and 5:

"For thou art my rock and my fortress; therefore for thy name's sake lead me and guide me. Pull me out of the net that they have laid privily for me; for thou art my strength. Into thine hand I commit my spirit: Thou hast redeemed me, Oh Lord God of truth!!!"

My meditations continued until I heard the Sergeant Major shouting from outside the shack! "Where's the skipper?" I popped my head out and replied, "What do you want?" Pappy came over, still shouting, "Regiment still has no word on the ETA of Arc Light. I think we'd better tell everyone to get in their holes…NOW! I estimate the Arc Light should be here in about forty-five minutes." I agreed! The Sergeant Major grabbed the three soaked and bedraggled company runners present. "Pass the word…keep digging…everyone stay in their holes."

Then he shouted, "Skipper, it's about time we got into our fox-holes too!" I was almost as unenthusiastic about getting hit above ground as I was about diving into a deep, muddy water-filled hole. However, Sergeant Major's admonishments prevailed…I dove in, wet and covered all over with that red pervasive Vietnam mud slurry, praying…praying.

0535: Then, as if it were an eternity…it got very quiet…then an enormous shwisshhhh, much like air passing through a large wind tunnel. A pause and the cacophony of noise like clapping thunder over and over again. Then it was over! I had been bombed before by the enemy in WWII, but nothing as fearful as this. I got on the sound power phone to the COs asking for a report. It took a long anxious hour before results came in. No, not one Marine was hurt…shaken but no injuries. Miracle of miracles, the lucky but errant Echo Company Patrol had slithered into our lines just about a half an hour before the deluge of bombs. They had accomplished their mission.

Thank God for His deliverance of my Marines. The war went on from there. At about 0700 I followed Echo Company into the target area for a target assessment. The report was one of bitter irony.

"The valley floor was churned up, much like a plowed field. About twenty chewed up NVA bodies were discovered. In one cave, our people shot a group of NVA soldiers trying to escape to the east towards Laos. The main force was nowhere to be seen."

To me it was another day in Vietnam…a massive expenditure of energy and materials with a modicum of results. The next several days 2/5 experienced some additional hairy adventures. We got into some real pitched battles with the NVA. By the time this Operation ended, I'd lose five killed in action and thirty-five wounded. This still pains me to even think of. I will never forget all of the fine young Americans who gave their ALL in an unpopular war in a far away place…to no avail!…

The above is a telling example of God's unswerving attempt to show me the way when I was still too blind to see. The Lord Jesus Christ protected me from death, even when I felt like an undeserving sinner. Little did I know then about God's saving grace. This was August 1966 and I didn't really wise up until 1972, when I finally saw the light!

It wasn't until I became a "born again Christian" in 1972 that the healing process commenced in my body and soul. Before my conversion, I was a "ritual Christian," meaning that I went to church, taught Sunday School and was even a Sunday School superintendent, when no one else wanted the job. After feeling "holy" on Sunday, I would revert to my sinful nature the rest of the week. Yes, I was a true but misguided practitioner of several deadly sins: pride, greed and lust, all woven into an alcoholic makeup. For years, in my blindness, I never realized that our Lord was sending me a message, "Wise up, Walter, before it is too late." Finally I came to terms with understanding why the Lord spared me. Putting my faith in the Lord turned the key to unraveling a terrible knot in my stomach. On many occasions, I tried to drown out this burning gut of guilt with alcohol. It was almost a form of grieving. It never worked and I didn't realize it until I supplanted booze with the spiritual power of the Lord in my heart.

SCRIPTURE: *If any man is in Christ, he is a new creation; old things are passed away, behold all things are become new. – 2 Corinthians 5.17*

PRAYER: *Lord God, if I am a "ritual Christian" only, help me to get real and personally take Jesus Christ into my innermost being. Amen.*

✯   ✯   ✯

In the name of the President of the United States, the Commanding General, Fleet Marine Force, Pacific takes pleasure in presenting the LEGION OF MERIT to

COLONEL WALTER MOORE
UNITED STATES MARINE CORPS

for service as set forth in the following

CITATION:
"For exceptionally meritorious conduct in the performance of outstanding service as the Commanding Officer of the Second Battalion, Fifth Marines, First Marine Division from 24 May to 1 September 1966 and subsequently as the Assistant Chief of Staff, G-5, from 2 September 1966 to 7 February 1967, in connection with operations against insurgent communist (Viet Cong) forces in the Republic of Vietnam. As the Commanding Officer of the Second Battalion, Fifth Marines, Colonel MOORE, then a Lieutenant Colonel, demonstrated exceptional leadership and judgment in the performance of his demanding duties. Skillfully, he initiated an aggressive program of patrols in his battalion's Tactical Area of Responsibility which eliminated Viet Cong influence and restricted the enemy's movements. Exhibiting outstanding tactical skill and determination, Colonel MOORE led his battalion in numerous successful operations, including Operations Colorado and Apache. Tirelessly, he supervised the training of his unit leaders in the use of supporting arms fire and constantly sought to improve the effective tactical employment of his units despite conditions of difficult terrain and adverse weather. With enthusiasm and foresight, Colonel MOORE planned and supervised

his battalion's Civic Action Program, conducting countless medical and civic action patrols into distant villages and hamlets to assist and treat the Vietnamese civilians. Through his program of increased civil affairs activity, he succeeded in winning many areas away from Viet Cong influence. Additionally, Colonel MOORE established the first Combined Action Unit within the Regimental Area of Responsibility. Re-assigned as the Assistant Chief of Staff, G-5, on 2 September 1966, Colonel MOORE directed the Civic Action Programs throughout the DaNang Tactical Area of Responsibility. With resourcefulness and tireless determination, he coordinated the efforts of the United States and Vietnamese governments in providing care for more than 2,200 refugees released from Viet Cong control during Operation Mississippi. On 24 December 1966, when an airliner crashed in a nearby village, killing and injuring many Vietnamese civilians and demolishing numerous homes, Colonel MOORE proceeded immediately to the crash site where he assumed command of the rescue efforts. As soon as rescue operations were completed, he coordinated the reconstruction of the damaged village. Working tirelessly, Colonel MOORE supervised the successful completion of the reconstruction and repair projects well ahead of schedule, contributing to the morale of the Vietnamese people and advancing the civic action programs in the Republic of Vietnam. His exemplary conduct and aggressiveness throughout, contributed immeasurably to the successful accomplishment of the division's mission. By his exceptional professional skill, bold initiative, and unswerving devotion to duty, Colonel MOORE upheld the highest traditions of the Marine Corps and of the United States Naval Service."

Colonel MOORE is authorized to wear the Combat "V".

FOR THE PRESIDENT,
F.C. THARIN
MAJOR GENERAL, U.S. MARINE CORPS

Lt. Frank Reasoner,
USMC, 1962

Sally Reasoner, Frank's widow, receiving Frank's posthumous Medal of Honor from
Secretary of the Navy Paul Nitze

Three

FRANK REASONER'S PREMONITION

by Bob Boardman

*When the day that he must go hence was come, many accom-
panied him to the riverside, into which as he went, he said:
"Death, where is thy sting?" And as he went down deeper, he
said: "Grave, where is thy victory?" So he passed over, and all
the trumpets sounded for him on the other side*
> — John Bunyan, The Pilgrim's Progress

Frank Reasoner, lieutenant of Marines, was close to his appointed time. He had a premonition that he would not return from Vietnam alive. Though every living being has an appointed time to die, very few are given a premonition of their appointment. Only the Living God knows the precise place and time. It might be today. It might be early in life, or at the end of our normally allotted seventy years—or in between.

Reasoner was part of a special unit in Vietnam, the Third Reconnaissance Battalion. This unit fought for about four and a half years, from 1965 to 1970. The various battalion recon teams, which varied from three- or four-man units to company size, accomplished the following:

> *They sighted 37,049 enemy and accounted for 2,534 enemy killed in action (KIA), 2,712 VC either wounded or suspected KIA, and 76 individuals captured who were either known enemy or suspected to be so.*
> — Lawrence Vetter, *Never Without Heroes*
> (New York: Ballantine Books, 1996) p. 2

The approximately 2,800 Marines who served at various times in Third Recon paid a tremendous price with their lives, their blood, sweat, tears and prayers: 1,121 Marines and 12 Navy Corpsmen were killed, wounded or missing (MIA). That comes to a 40 percent casualty rate.

Our nation honored her warrior sons in Third Recon by bestowing upon them four Medals of Honor, thirteen Navy Crosses and seventy-three Silver Stars. The entire battalion was awarded one Presidential Unit Citation, two Navy Unit Citations, one Meritorious Unit Citation and eleven battle stars for Vietnamese service.

Lawrence Vetter said this about those who were not individually rewarded: "*An even greater number were better honored by the respect of their peers.*" This respect is the element in any Armed Forces reunion that binds men together. It can never be bought at any price.

Frank Reasoner of Kellogg, Idaho, was one of the four men in Third Recon who was awarded the Medal of Honor (MOH). All four of these Marines, in separate actions, gave their lives sacrificially to save their comrades.

Tolman Udell Meyers (chapter 6) and Frank Reasoner were stationed together as lieutenants at Kaneohe, Hawaii, in the First Marine Brigade. They deployed on an exercise on APA 248 USS *Paul Revere*, which included training on Okinawa. Udell and Frank became good friends. Later they met in Vietnam when both served in the Third Reconnaissance Battalion. Here are Udell's words in a letter that describe that unusual premonition that gripped Reasoner's heart:

Several days before Frank was killed, he was conducting rubber boat assault training with his A Company on China Beach, Danang East. It had been awhile since we had seen each other so I looked forward to this reunion. Frank was always upbeat, enthusiastic, exuding a confidence that was contagious.

When we met on that beach, I was not prepared for what I saw. His countenance had fallen. His usual exuberance of social grace was replaced with expressions both somber and sullen. I asked if he was all right, and he replied, "I'm not going home." I responded by saying, "None of us know when we'll be going home, as our orders are indefinite."

"No," he countered, "I'm not going home alive."

I tried to brush off his comment and encourage him in every way I could possibly think of, but to no avail. I sensed that he had a certainty about the matter based on something he knew and did not want to discuss.

After Frank's death I learned that he knew weeks in advance that his company had been tasked with conducting some patrols that were extremely high risk. Because of his concern for the lives of his Marines conducting these operations, he insisted on accompanying them into harm's way.

On that fateful day, 12 July 1965, Frank Reasoner, married and father of a baby boy eight months old, led an advance patrol deep into a Viet Cong district where they came under heavy sniper and machine gun fire and were pinned down.

Lieutenant Reasoner's Medal of Honor award, reading in part, best tells the story of these valiant men:

The reconnaissance patrol led by Lt. Reasoner…came under heavy fire from an estimated 50 to 100 Viet Cong firing machine guns, automatic rifles and carbines from concealed positions.

*He exposed himself to machine gun and small arms fire
and shouted encouragement to his men. He then quickly
organized a base of fire to support the assault on the enemy
positions.*

*Within minutes one of the Marines with Lt. Reasoner was
wounded. In the face of intensive fire, Lt. Reasoner sought to
cover the evacuation of the wounded man, himself killing at
least two of the Viet Cong and effectively silencing an automatic weapons position. As casualties began to mount, his
radio operator was wounded.*

*After crawling a considerable distance, the radio operator
was hit a second time and could move no further. Realizing
that the man could not survive in the heavy enemy fire
sweeping the open ground between him and the radio operator, Lt. Reasoner courageously leaped to his feet, shouting to
the man that he would carry him out. He ran through the
grazing machine gun fire but was struck and fell mortally
wounded at his radioman's side.*

*Inspired by his actions, his men killed 16 more of the
enemy, knocked out the machine-gun, and, heeding the
Lieutenant's last words, got their wounded comrades safely out.*

Frank Stanley Reasoner was, in Marine parlance, a "Mustang."
That is, he was a Marine enlisted man before becoming an officer.
After his graduation from high school in Kellogg, Idaho, in June
1955, he enlisted in the Corps at the age of seventeen.

After time in the Marines, he received an appointment to West
Point. Upon graduation he was welcomed back into the Marine
Corps by two Marine major generals as a second lieutenant.
Ultimately this outstanding young warrior became the first Marine
officer to receive the Medal of Honor for his valiance in Vietnam.

Frank Reasoner's life, sacrificial action and death so impacted all
of Third Recon Battalion that they named their area Camp
Reasoner. Underneath the sign over the camp entrance was this
inscription, *"Greater love hath no man."* This is part of the immor-
tal words of the Savior recorded in the Gospels.

*Greater love hath no man than this, that a man lay down his
life for his friends.* — *John 15.13*

What is it that makes a man like Reasoner tick? What motivates his inner life to enable him to lay down his life willingly for his comrades?

Here are further thoughts from fellow officer Tolman Udell Meyers. His words give us clues to the commitment and faithfulness of his friend:

Knowing of the grave danger these patrols faced, he could not order them to go unless he went with them, shared their fate and assisted in any way he could. He gave his last full measure of devotion in a life-giving effort to save the lives of his men.

That day I visited him on China Beach, he was envisioning with certainty the high price of command and true leadership. And though it shook him to his very soul, it did not move nor weaken his resolve to go into the Valley of the Shadow of Death, face the foe, and care for those in his charge no matter the cost, by life or by death.

Such was the courage and commitment of Frank Reasoner, the personification of what it means to be Semper Fidelis, Always Faithful, to God and country.

— T.U. Meyers

Reasoner's mother, Daisy, and siblings, Marilyn, Larry and Janice, and stepfather, Jim Curry, were God-fearing, strong, praying people. This factor no doubt laid a strong moral-spiritual foundation in his young life.

Another unmistakable part of the strong premonition of pending death in the young Marine's life was revealed in a visit of Frank to his wife, Sally, to see his infant son on a short break from Vietnam.

In an emotion-filled tender moment, he requested of Sally that if he didn't come back from the war and she remarried, would she please not change his son Mickey's last name. Sally graciously granted that, one of his last requests. It seems crystal clear that Frank was mysteriously well aware of his appointment with the Angel of Death.

Again, the words of Frank's personal friend help us gain insights into his life just before his premonitory death.

While I never heard Frank witness or testify with regard to assurance of his salvation, the fruit of the Spirit described in Galatians 5.22,23 was evident.

Udell describes how the challenge of Frank's death deeply affected his own spiritual life:

Before Frank's death I had not been very vocal about my faith with my fellow Marines. I can, therefore, relate to those who keep a low profile as to being in the Lord's army. It is very possible that Frank was likewise keeping private about his faith.

Following Frank's death, I was thereby motivated to not merely be content with just having assurance of my own salvation, but to share the Good News with my fellow Marines and especially those in my command.

— T.U. Meyers

After reading Frank Reasoner's story, many of us can acknowledge that his premonition uniquely came from God. Frank's sacrificial death has, no doubt, in God's sovereignty, impacted many more people than if he lived a full, normal seventy years.

SCRIPTURE: *I most solemnly say to you, unless a grain of wheat falls into the ground and dies, it remains a single grain. But if it does die, it yields a great harvest.* — *John 12.24*

PRAYER: *Whether by a prolonged life or an "early" death, help me, O Holy One, to impact others for Your glory. In Jesus' sacrificial life and death I pray. Amen.*

Four

THE CHIEF OF STAFF

by Bob Boardman

We are always on the Anvil; by trials God is shaping us for higher things.

— Henry Ward Beecher

I still chuckle about my chance encounter with Colonel Amor LeRoy Sims, USMC, almost sixty years ago on Goodenough Island. I don't think, as a private, I had ever seen a full Marine colonel, let alone been "addressed" by one. I had been in the Corps less than one year. In my nineteen-year-old mind, a Marine colonel was sort of like the vice president of the US.

Colonel Sims was the First Marine Division Chief of Staff, which means he carried out the administrative duties for the Division Commander, who at that time was Major General William H.

Rupertus. The Reinforced First Marine Division had about 22,000 men and so the Chief of Staff's responsibilities were quite extensive. You would think he wouldn't want to take time to tangle with a lowly Marine private from Salem, Oregon!

The Division had just moved by mass-produced Liberty Ships from Melbourne, Australia in preparation for the invasion of Cape Gloucester, New Britain. Using Liberty Ships for troop transports meant the "heads" (toilets), showers (salt water), and galleys were built on the weather decks. In stormy weather it resulted in chaos. Because of the tropical heat, we mostly slept topside on hard steel decks using life vests for pillows.

After Australia, the staging and training areas for the coming invasion were in three main locations. The Fifth Marine Regiment reinforced was sent to Milne Bay, in the eastern part of New Guinea; the Seventh Regiment to Oro Bay, past Milne on the northwest coast; the Engineer Regiment Headquarters and Division Headquarters were sent to Goodenough Island, of the French-controlled De Entrecasteaux Group, about eighty miles equidistant from both Milne and Oro Bays.

Our C Company, First Tank Battalion ended up on Goodenough where we cleared our campsite out of thick jungle and pitched our eight-man tents in orderly rows. Parts of Goodenough were some of the most beautiful island paradises in the world, although fraught with some vicious looking snakes that we encountered.

One sweltering day our C Company was ordered to provide a large working party to clear the jungle for Division Headquarters, several miles away. The natives would then construct thatched roof structures for the Commanding General and his staff, which included Colonel Sims.

About fifty of us were transported by large, ten-wheel trucks to the site and told we would be picked up at the end of the day. We toiled all day in the hot, steamy jungles with machetes, axes and shovels, clearing the jungle. At the end of the day we anticipated being hauled back to C Company for a dip in a nearby jungle stream, followed by hot chow. No trucks showed.

Finally we began to straggle down the dusty, crude jungle road with tools slung over our shoulders, tired, dirty and beat, trudging the several miles back to our Company area.

Along came a jeep slowly making its way through this grimy, scattered group. The front seat next to the driver was empty so I put out my thumb to hitch a ride. The lighting was such that I couldn't see the lone figure in the back seat. The jeep obligingly stopped and I jogged over, happy to ride while my buddies trudged on.

I had just placed one leg in the jeep when I saw that the figure in the back was a colonel. I began to back away when his sharp voice shattered my good fortune:

"Alright, get in! I'm taking you to your unit! Didn't you know I've put out an order that there's to be no thumbing on this island?"

"No sir," I stammered.

"What is your outfit? I'm taking you to your company commander!"

A couple of my buddies had also jogged over to the jeep, eager to share the ride. They heard the colonel royally dressing me down and were able to slowly back away and escape. I didn't dare wave and couldn't now gloat as we slowly passed the trudging work party.

Amor LeRoy Sims. *Amor* means "love," *LeRoy* means "The King." The colonel was the epitome of "spit and polish," with freshly starched and pressed khakis and highly polished dress shoes, even there in the jungle. I'm sure he also carried a swagger stick.

Arriving in C Company, he dressed down our warrant officer in the company tent, who did not rise, because of the poor lighting, when the colonel entered. I was put on report and received twenty hours EPD (extra police duty) — digging garbage pits and other coolie labor.

As a Marine private, I had many lessons to learn in life. I was on the anvil and the Chief of Staff was the hammer to shape me a bit more into the man and Marine God had in mind. Not knowing the colonel's order was no excuse. God uses pain, hardship and trauma, small or great, to conform us to Christ and to ultimately glorify His matchless name.

SCRIPTURE: *My son, refrain from thinking lightly of the discipline the Lord inflicts, and giving up when you are corrected by Him. For He disciplines everyone He loves, and chastises every son whom He heartily receives. You must submit to discipline…* — *Hebrews 12.5,6,7*

PRAYER: *From time to time and from season to season, as You, Lord, put me on the Anvil, give me an accepting, thankful heart through the pain. Amen.*

Five

THE BLACK ANGEL

by Bob Boardman

Do not remain neglectful of hospitality to strangers,
for by it some have entertained angels without knowing it.
—Hebrews 13.2

He spotted me on the crowded ward of the hospital ship, USS *Solace*. This black man, clad in his clean, blue Navy dungarees, appeared to be a member of the ship's crew. He made his way through the crowded bunks of wounded Marines and sailors, came up to me with an engaging smile, stuck out his hand and said:

"My name's so & so—good to meet you. What's your name
and where are you from?"

My right hand was bandaged so I gave him my left. I tried to tell him my name, but no sound came out, not even a light whisper. Every day I tried to make a sound, form a word, but nothing came forth—only the air from labored breathing through the tracheotomy tube inserted into my throat on the battlefield.

The hospital ship was riding low in the water, filled with wounded from the last great land battle of WWII. Over one quarter of a million were killed on both sides. The Army, Navy and Marines had suffered tremendous casualties in defeating the fanatical Japanese Imperial Forces on Okinawa in 1945.

This particular hospital ship, the USS *Solace*, was coming from the island of Guam heading for San Francisco. Many of us who were wounded in Okinawa were sent by sea and air to Guam before being trans-shipped to the US.

This black, new-found friend hesitated beside my bed and then went down to the foot and read my name and casualty information from the hospital tag: *"Boardman, Robert R., gunshot wounds, neck, larynx and hand, Okinawa, 17 June 1945."*

I was a Sherman tank driver in C Company, First Tank Battalion, First Marine Division that fateful morning just four days before the end of the battle. Two of our tanks sustained severe casualties from Japanese anti-tank fire. We who escaped were soon gunned down by Japanese snipers.

The ship's crewman, whose name I can't remember, was attracted to my bunk in that crowded hospital ward because he spotted me reading a Gideon-issued New Testament.

I was a relatively new believer, having put my faith in Jesus Christ near New Guinea about eighteen months before Okinawa, my third battle. On Cape Gloucester, New Britain, I knew that God wanted me to share with others, as my life's vocation, the Open Secret that God loves them.

Now I found myself with no voice, not even a faint whisper. Several questions loomed in my mind as I tried to read the New Testament given to me on Guam by Joe Alvarez, a close buddy and wounded C Company comrade.

How can I serve God with no voice? My God has all power. He could have prevented this and protected me. Why did He have to let this happen?

Into every one of our lives comes suffering in one of its myriad forms. No one is immune. It is very difficult when we first enter its doors and peer into the dark room of trial, to see and understand any worthwhile purpose.

The black crewman seemed to ponder how he could best help me. Then he reached over and took the New Testament out of my hand. In my weakened condition and with the aforementioned questions looming large, I wasn't getting much out of the book, even though I was silently praying for God's help to understand.

My new friend opened up the pages of the book that a few months before had revealed to me the answers to life, death, my wrongdoings and the gift of eternal life. *"Here, Bob, read this chapter. I'll come back and visit you tomorrow."*

There are several major milestones in each of our lives during our pilgrimage. These are turning points, critical times of decision. Our response and decision determine the entire remaining direction of the way we will go. Aboard that hospital ship was just such a critical milestone for me.

The chapter that was opened by this kind sailor was Romans 8. I read and reread it many times. It didn't tell me *why* God allowed this affliction in my life. But it did tell me that God knew all about it and that if I trusted Him it would all work together for my good and for God's glory. Romans 8 also told me that there wasn't anything that could separate me from God's love, despite my limitations and weaknesses.

Was this a black angel that God sent in answer to my heart-cry for help? It could have been. Or else it was a believer who was Spirit-led who opened his Bible in the right place in time of great need in my life. Someday I will know for sure. Until then, to me, he is *God's Black Angel.*

☆　☆　☆

SCRIPTURE: *The Spirit is helping us in our weakness, for we do not know how to pray as we should, but the Spirit Himself pleads for us with unspeakable yearnings. And He who searches our hearts knows what the Spirit thinks, for He pleads for His people in accordance with God's will. Yes, we know that all things go on working together for the good of those who keep on loving God, who are called in accordance with God's purpose. — Romans 8.26,27,28*

PRAYER: *Thank you, Father, for full assurance that no force in heaven or earth, including death, can separate me from Your love, in Christ Jesus my Lord. Amen.*

Lt. T. Udell Meyers, USMC, immediately following fire-fight, Vietnam, 1965

Udell Meyers and 3rd Recon buddy Harry Rogers at DC Reunion. Udell is Navigator staff in Quantico, Virginia.

Six

Surviving an Ambush
Tolman Udell Meyers' Story

By Bob Boardman

Lessons on Courage, Compassion and Service

Pay not attention to those who would keep you far from fire; you want to prove yourself a man of courage. If there are opportunities, expose yourself conspicuously. As for real danger, it is everywhere in war.

— Napoleon, 2 February 1806

In early October of 1965, Marine Aerial Reconnaissance sorties detected a buildup of communist forces in a section of dense jungle twenty miles southwest of the US airbase near Danang, South Vietnam. Marines of the Third Reconnaissance Battalion, called "The Eyes and Ears of the Third Marine Division," were tasked to conduct the onsite surveillance and report on the strength and activity of the enemy.

These "Lean and Mean Recon Marines," as they were respectfully called, possessed the expertise essential to carrying out missions in the enemy's domain. Their missions, though usually successful, were not without sacrifice. The per capita casualty rates were high in comparison to those of other combat arms units. For this reason, all Recon Marines were volunteers. Their camaraderie was *par excellence* and disciplinary problems minimal.

They traveled light, giving priority to the combat essentials. While on patrol, one meal a day was the normal fare. The C-rations, or "rats" in Marine jargon, was a one-meal cardboard box containing small cans of meat, fruit (if you were lucky), pound cake or white bread, and a small tin of jam or peanut butter and crackers. On the eve of the mission, code named Operation Trailblazer, chaplains were flown to the Recon Base Camp to conduct Divine Services. Although intended to provide solace for the soul, most considered it a harbinger of mishap, an ill omen.

The final hour before the UH34D helicopters (helos) arrived to take them into "harm's way," the Marines were busily attending to personal needs, checking weapons and gear, or writing letters to loved ones. Some read their Gideon New Testaments and prayed.

Lieutenant T. Udell Meyers of Shipman, Illinois, the platoon leader of Second Platoon D Company, was having some quiet time with the Lord. He had placed his trust in Christ for salvation before coming into the Corps, and with each patrol felt one step closer to death and nearer to God. As he sat reading the Scriptures, Corporal James Malone of Kosciusko, Mississippi, presented a message to the lieutenant from the company commander, Captain Patrick Collins. Typical of the "Skipper's" orders, the message was brief and to the point: **"Take Dobbs, you're gonna need him!"**

Corporal John Dobbs of Texas, was an outstanding Recon Marine who had been wounded twice since arriving in Vietnam seven months earlier. In spite of his protests, Udell had assigned him to remain in base camp for "light duty" and convalescence.

Meyers dispatched Malone to tell Dobbs to "saddle up!" Corporal Malone cracked a smile and replied, "He's all ready, sir." As Udell was about to dismiss Malone, the corporal pointed to the lieutenant's Bible and asked, "Is that your lucky rabbit's foot, sir?" Udell dismissed the veiled note of sarcasm and insubordinate slight and tried to answer in a measured and meaningful manner. "No, Corporal," the lieutenant replied, "That is God's Holy Word, and through it and my response to Christ, I have assurance of eternal life. We could both die on this mission, but I know where I'm going! Do you?"

Although the corporal made no audible response, his body language bespoke his uncertainty and his unwillingness to continue the discussion. Udell dismissed Malone and then prayed for yet another opportunity to share the Gospel with him before it was too late.

Operation Trailblazer got underway as scheduled and proceeded without incident until day four when enemy ambushes resulted in the wounding of four Marines and the death of one enemy. The next day Lieutenant Meyers, as the lead element, led his platoon of twenty-two men. By midday he assessed the situation and perceived that the terrain and weather favored the enemy. The time foreseen by Captain Collins was at hand, and Corporal Dobbs was moved to the "tip of the spear," the Point Man.

Within minutes of resuming the patrol, the ominous silence was shattered when a twelve-man enemy unit opened up with several bursts from their AK-47 assault rifles. Corporal Dobbs, vigilantly performing at the "point," had detected the enemy, forcing them to trigger their ambush prematurely. Four rounds from their initial burst ripped through his chest and abdomen.

Meyers and his men immediately hurled grenades on the enemy position, gained fire superiority, and assaulted. From the depth of each man's inner being came a spontaneous scream, a war cry as ancient as war itself. The Lieutenant saw muzzle flashes fifty feet to his front and at the same instant felt the full force of several rounds slam into his body. Four rounds struck him in the right arm and hand, three hit his M-14 rifle and rendered it inoperable, another pierced a grenade strapped to his ammo belt, but miraculously it did not detonate. Yet another round struck a 16mm reconnaissance camera in his breast pocket and deflected.

The impact of the volley spun the lieutenant around and knocked him to the ground. As he struggled to remove his .45 caliber pistol from its holster, another burst of automatic weapon fire streaked over his head and slammed into Corporal Malone. Meyers and Navy Corpsman "Doc" Ralph E. Bratcher, of La Follet, Tennessee, rushed to Malone's side. His right arm had been nearly severed at the elbow. As the "Doc" tended to Malone, Udell grabbed Corporal Malone's rifle and locked in a full magazine. The "Doc" insisted on taking a look at Udell's wounds. What remained of his thumb was grotesquely dangling by a thread of skin. Bratcher reluctantly complied with the lieutenant's order to cut it off, "surgically" removing it with his field knife.

As Udell rose up to rejoin the fray, Malone grabbed him by the arm and cried out, "Pray for me, I'm dying and I'm not ready to die." The lieutenant shouted a prayer, "Oh God, help him!", then tore himself free and pressed the assault.

Meyers continues his incredible story of bravery and courage in the face of intense and overwhelming odds:

> *By the time we overran their position and took the ridge, we had seven wounded. Both Dobbs and Malone were bleeding profusely and needed to be evacuated to the nearest aid station—ASAP!*
>
> *My radioman, L.Cpl. George Ortel, succeeded in contacting two Air Force "Huskies," helos with winch cable capability. They arrived within 30 minutes and hoisted the wounded out through the dense jungle canopy, all the while being fired upon by snipers that had taken up positions in the treetops.*

Marine helo-gunships soon arrived to give the "huskies" covering fire as they transported their bloody cargo to C-Med near Danang. Dobbs, Malone and Meyers were treated and held overnight and transferred the next morning to the USAF hospital at Clark Field in the Philippines.

Tom Hash, an acquaintance of Udell's, learned of the lieutenant's medevac to Clark Hospital. Tom was serving as the director of the Overseas Christian Servicemen's Center there. He rounded up several airmen and they went to the ward to visit the wounded.

As they gathered around Meyers' bed, they sang hymns, read Scriptures, and prayed for his complete recovery. They didn't know that Udell had been told just before their arrival that he was scheduled to have his arm amputated the next morning.

At 0300, medics came to prep Udell, not for surgery as expected, but for a mcdevac to Tripler Army Hospital in Oahu, Hawaii, where new antibiotics spared his arm.

Soon Udell's wife, Janet, and two-year-old daughter, Holly, were united with him in a joyous reunion in Hawaii. In the vernacular of the Marines serving in Vietnam, mainland USA was "The World," and Hawaii was "Paradise." And so it seemed for Udell and his family upon being united.

Toward the end of Udell's recovery process, the US Naval Services rightfully awarded him the Bronze Star with "Valor V" for his incredible courage.

In the name of the President of the United States, the Commanding General, Fleet Marine Force, Pacific takes pleasure in presenting the BRONZE STAR MEDAL to

FIRST LIEUTENANT TOLMAN UDELL MEYERS
UNITED STATES MARINE CORPS

for service as set forth in the following
CITATION:
"For heroic achievement in connection with operations against insurgent communist (Viet Cong) forces while serving as a Platoon Commander with Company D, Third Reconnaissance Battalion, Third Marine Division near DaNang, Republic of Vietnam. On 23 October 1965, First Lieutenant MEYERS' lead squad was taken under fire by an enemy force. Moving forward with the remainder of his platoon, First Lieutenant MEYERS quickly assessed the situation, deployed his platoon and moved forward along the route. After proceeding a short distance his platoon was taken under heavy enemy fire, the initial burst severing First Lieutenant MEYERS' right thumb and wounding two of his men. Despite the intense pain from his wound, he refused evacuation, moved to the front of his platoon and boldly led them in a vigorous frontal assault through the enemy positions, which resulted in four guerrillas killed. Maintaining complete control over his men in consolidating their position, he gave encouragement to the other wounded

and saw to their evacuation before he finally allowed himself to be treated and evacuated. First Lieutenant MEYERS' inspiring leadership and courageous actions throughout were in keeping with the highest traditions of the United States Naval Service."

First Lieutenant MEYERS is authorized to wear the Combat "V".

FOR THE PRESIDENT,
V. H. KRULAK
LIEUTENANT GENERAL, US MARINE CORPS
COMMANDING

☆   ☆   ☆

Lieutenant Meyers served another eighteen months on active duty, attaining the rank of captain before entering the Standby-Reserves.

When the American forces commenced pulling out of Vietnam in the fall of 1972, Udell returned as a civilian and distributed 100,000 Scripture booklets printed in the Vietnamese language. He traversed the length and breadth of South Vietnam distributing the Word of God to South Vietnamese soldiers, refugees, lepers, orphans, and communist prisoners of war. The return to this foreign land, where the trauma of combat had left its indelible mark on his body, mind and soul, was for Meyers an awesome and invaluable journey.

Here in his own words is a summary of his feelings:

When it became apparent that the war would be lost to the communists, my spirit was vexed. Thousands of Americans and South Vietnamese had sacrificed for a just and noble cause, yet were denied a victory. Like so many veterans of the war, I had grown to love these freedom loving people, and lamented their inevitable fate. Also, through my growing appreciation for God's mercy and grace in my own life, I had developed a compassion for the lost souls of my enemy. I departed Vietnam Thanksgiving Day and was genuinely thankful for the privilege God had given me to share His help from above.

In the years that have followed his Vietnam experience, Udell and Janet have ministered to US Armed Forces personnel and their families in the Philippines, Guam, England, and currently at the Marine

Corps Base in Quantico, Virginia. They minister to Marines, both on and off the base, in cooperation with the chaplains. Through The Rally Point, a Service Center facility they established in the liberty town of Quantico, they minister to the adults and children of the civilian community and to the Marines and their families.

In the heat of battle Udell's assurance of eternal life brought peace to his trembling soul, and a compassion for those who were facing death and dying without it. It was in the midst of combat that he heard God's clarion call:

The fire of my passion for military ministry was ignited by the pathetic plea of Cpl. James Malone, "Pray for me. I'm dying and I'm not ready to die!"

☆   ☆   ☆

SCRIPTURE: *For God hath not given us the spirit of fear, but of power, and of love, and of a sound mind. —2 Timothy 1.7*

PRAYER: *Lord, grant me the same bravery and courage under fire— and the same spirit of forgiveness and service to both friend and enemy, at home and abroad. In Jesus' name, Amen.*

* Cpl. James Malone not only survived the ambush, but shortly thereafter placed his trust in Christ. He was promoted to the rank of sergeant and medically discharged. He resides with his wife, Shelby, in Kosciusko, Mississippi. As fellow Marines and comrades, Udell and James are mutually committed to serve the Lord as long as they have breath. Semper Fidelis!

★ II ★

The Battlefield Way

After one hour of viewing the battlefield on Okinawa, Lt. Gen. Simon Bolivar Buckner, USA, confidently prepared to depart to visit another unit. At this moment the expert Japanese artillery officer gave word to fire and laid five scarce, precious rounds into this tempting target.

General Buckner's appointment with death had arrived. One of those five shells hit one of the boulders, showering chips, flying shrapnel and coral fragments, some of which dug into the general's chest and abdomen. The profuse bleeding could not be stanched and in ten minutes he was dead.

With so much death everywhere, this seemed to some "not inappropriate." And it was a matter of inches, in the battlefield way. None of the officers accompanying him were scratched. Like so many of his men, the commander had been dealt a dose of combat's vast store of random bad luck.

— Feifer

From *Unforgettable Men in Unforgettable Times*

Lieutenant Commander David Taft, USN, Vietnam, 1966

Capt. Taft, First Marine Division surgeon, now retired and residing in Seattle, Washington.

Seven

THE SURGEON WHO DID NOT WANT THE MEDAL OF HONOR

by Bob Boardman

Courage is fear holding on a minute longer.
— General George S. Patton, Jr.

Still a young boy, David Taft was at the movies in Ames, Iowa with his father and brother John watching *Sergeant York* when the bombing of Pearl Harbor took place on 7 December 1941. He vividly remembers his father's distress and anger from the unprovoked attack.

A few months later he received a beautiful shoulder patch from a neighbor whose son was a Marine, emblazoned with the Southern Cross and a large red "One" with Guadalcanal written on it. The patch was the emblem of the famed First Marine Division who were primarily responsible in the early stages of WWII for stopping the Japanese in their southeasterly drive toward Australia and New Zealand.

Little did David know at that time that he would end up years later in Vietnam in that very same First Marine Division. Nor did he know that in the division as a young thirty-four-year-old skilled Navy surgeon he would receive the nation's second highest award, the Navy Cross.

The greatest challenge to David Taft's own courage, coolness and skill would be to remove a live 2.75-inch rocket embedded in a young Marine's knee joint. The precariousness and required skill of that surgery would mark David Taft for life.

With many people it seems as though all of life's difficult circumstances, training and discipline unknowingly point us toward one traumatic event that brands us for a lifetime. This event or circumstance is beyond our knowledge or control and choosing. It must come from the God who controls all circumstances. It seems this was true in David Taft's life. Vietnam awaited him.

Taft graduated from medical school in 1959 and in his own words, *"We cheerfully went off to our internships thinking we were pretty hot stuff. Fifteen minutes into my internship at Ohio State University Hospital, I quickly learned how much I didn't know!"*

In his surgical residency at Ohio State, he had the good fortune to train under Dr. Robert Zollinger, whom David described as *"one of the most fascinating, slave-driving, hard-working and talented surgeons in the US."* In six years under the tutelage of Dr. Zollinger, Taft progressed from a green intern to a well-trained and capable surgeon that had cared for a large number of complex trauma patients. He had learned enough neurosurgery to do craniotomies for intracranial bleeding, was adept at lung, heart and vascular surgery, and could carry out all the abdominal and head and neck cases that make up the range of general surgical procedures.

During further training at the Royal Infirmary in Edinburgh, Scotland in 1956 and 1965, David met and pursued Miss Sheila Blackwood, who is now his wife and *"best friend of 34 years."*

One of Taft's mentors, a surgeon in the European Theater in WWII, told him that *"a surgeon's training is not finished until he has served as a combat surgeon."* David wanted to go with the best, the US Marines, and to get in on the action as soon as possible before the Vietnam war was over. Through Dr. Zollinger's influence and after a basic physical exam, he was soon sworn into the US Navy as a lieutenant commander.

"*Dr. Zollinger was amused that I thought it necessary to try so hard to go to Vietnam as he didn't think the volunteer line was very long. He was right!*" Taft mused. He was soon destined for hazardous duty with the Marine unit whose patch with the Southern Cross had been given him as a young boy.

On 1 October 1966 Taft arrived in Vietnam and was posted in Chu Lai to the First Medical Battalion, First Marine Division. He describes the scene:

I walked into the grubby little office, was cheerfully greeted as the new surgeon and was hustled across the road to the triage area teeming with patients. I selected the worst one and was steered to the operating room by a harried Navy Corpsman. My war had started three hours after my arrival in Vietnam.

Taft goes on to say:

In my next 15 months as part of the medical team I did the neurosurgery, chest surgery and vascular surgery, as well as general surgical cases, and even delivered a Vietnam lady of a fine baby boy while in the air inside a CH/34 helicopter. We probably had 150 corpsmen who tended to rotate with the field corpsmen.

That life-defining moment soon came into Dr. Taft's life, when on 27 August 1967, they brought in a severely wounded Marine with "something stuck in his knee." A roentgenogram soon showed that the object was a 2.75-inch live US rocket fired from one of our own helicopters. It had destroyed the kneecap, the vascular structures, as well as the articular surfaces, necessitating amputation above the knee.

Taft asked for one corpsman volunteer to assist him and then cleared the operating tent and the surrounding area. Daniel Henry bravely stepped forward, knowing that this could well cost him his life. Even though both medical men donned flak jackets for the operation, the jackets would likely have afforded little protection had the missile exploded.

A critical point in the operation was the sawing of the leg bone. The vibration of a power saw could well have detonated the rocket. Taft instead used a regular amputation saw, holding the rocket steady with his left hand. The tension both for those waiting outside the tent and for the three heroic men inside was indescribable. Many prayers were offered for the success and safety of this amazing venture.

God was merciful. The surgery was a success. The corpsman, Daniel Henry, was decorated with the Silver Star, our nation's third highest honor. Tragically he was killed a few months later in an enemy mortar attack.

The young Marine whose leg was amputated had a basketball scholarship at New York University. After the war, the school honored it, enabling him to become a successful CPA. Eventually he served in the state legislature. His life ended a few years ago by a heart attack.

David Taft has this to say about his fifteen-month Vietnam experience: *"An impressive observation we made in our care of casualties was the very low mortality rate once these wounded Marines reached our facility—and the fact that these casualties were often seen at our unit 30 to 45 minutes following the time of their wounding. No other war that I know of had this advantage of extremely rapid casualty evacuation to first class medical units, almost all carried out by helicopters."*

Again, the doctor shares how the war personally affected him: *"Surgeons through the ages have gone to any length to salvage the young that fight our wars. The personal trauma that any surgeon of significant combat surgery experiences will always leave wounds in him that never heal, but bleed each night when dreams arrive. Fortunately, the good that is done on the operating room table outweighs the occasional bad night or flashback. The results are worth it."*

THE REST OF THE STORY

Truth is indeed stranger than fiction! The amazing miracles that took place in this surgical story have not ended. Following the amputation, the intrepid Dr. Taft carried the leg outside the tent with the rocket still embedded. Marine ordnance personnel had dug a hole about two hundred yards away.

Taft very gently placed the leg in the hole and quickly returned to the operating tent to finish the operation. Before the surgery was completed, the rocket exploded before the ordnance crew could detonate it! Is this not the Lord's gracious and merciful timing?

Captain David Taft, USN, was rightfully awarded the Navy Cross. Why did he not want the most prestigious Medal of Honor? That would only have been awarded posthumously, if the rocket had exploded during the surgery!

☆ ☆ ☆

SCRIPTURE: *You, O Lord are a compassionate and gracious God, slow to anger, abounding in love and faithfulness. Turn to me and have mercy on me; grant Your strength to Your servant and save the son of your maidservant. — Psalm 86.15,16*

PRAYER: *Thank You, Lord, for your abundant mercy to these three stalwart men—and to me every day, even though I do not deserve it. Continue to provide that mercy for Your great name's sake. Amen.*

☆ ☆ ☆

Presentation of the Navy Cross to David A. Taft, USN:

Citation: For extraordinary heroism on 27 August 1967 while serving as a surgeon with the First Marine Division (Reinforced), FMF near Danang, Republic of Vietnam, in direct support of combat operations against communist insurgent (Viet Cong) forces. When a seriously wounded casualty with an "armed" 2.75-inch rocket imbedded in his left leg was brought by helicopter to the First Medical Battalion, Lieutenant Commander Taft carefully diagnosed the case, concluding that the knee joint, nerves and arteries in the area were destroyed and that surgical amputation was imperative and time was of the essence. Anticipating that the rocket might detonate at any moment, he immediately supervised the patient's emergency treatment and transfer to the operating room, setting an outstanding example of calmness and courage. He assisted with the administration of spinal anesthetic, which necessitated manipulating and positioning the victim several times. Lieutenant Commander Taft cleared the operating room of all personnel with the exception of the patient himself, and a Navy hospital corpsman, and then, with complete disregard for his own safety, coolly and competently performed the necessary surgery. By his expeditious treatment of the patient, his superior professional skill, and his unfaltering devotion to duty, Lieutenant Commander Taft undoubtedly saved the injured man's life, and was instrumental in removing the threat of death or injury from other personnel in the vicinity of the operating room, thereby upholding the highest traditions of the United States Naval Service.

Signed, Secretary of the Navy
Paul Ignatius

D.I. Bahde, USMC, 1943.
Photo shop in San Diego
furnished the dress blues just
out of Boot Camp.

D.I. Bahde today,
Kearney, Nebraska.

Eight

THE RICHES OF COMRADESHIP

The Alphabet Men of C Company
First Tank Battalion

D.I. Bahde's Story

by Bob Boardman

One of the lasting truths about being a soldier is that friend-ships formed with comrades in arms are the deepest and most enduring.

— General Fred Franks

In the last few months two more C Company comrades have taken the journey of no return. Glen "Old Man" Christensen, 87, an Alphabet Man who helped save my life in Okinawa, died quietly on 12 December 2000.

Orville Finley from Andrews, Texas may have stated it best when, toward the end of a long, full life, he wrote: "*Murph* [my nickname], *the friendships formed over in the Pacific in our C Company will never be equaled by any other."*

In Orville's last letter to me about two months before his number came up on 2 March 2000, he wrote this:

I found out earlier this year that I had a very bad heart. I went to Dallas and had a D.R. defibrillator implanted in my chest. When my heartbeat gets too fast this thing fires about 700 volts of electricity into my heart. Goldie and I were shopping at Sam's yesterday. We were walking along and I was pushing the cart and all of a sudden I felt like I just went to sleep. I fell to my knees and that thing kicked and it felt just like someone had hit me right across my chest with a baseball bat, but it brought me back.

Always proud to be your comrade

W.O. (Fin) Finley

How do you become true comrades with strangers from other parts of the country when you are suddenly thrown together? Sometimes the process is a bit traumatic. Here is Don I. Bahde's description of that process as we eventually became the closest of buddies. "D.I." saw me box in a boot camp smoker in December 1942. Here's his somewhat exaggerated description, read at my seventieth birthday. He called it *"The Making of a Friend"*:

After Boot Camp, the next time I saw this guy was at a Tank Training Camp at Jaques Farm. I bumped into him and probably lipped off. The next thing I remembered I was laying on my back with my glasses broken and wrapped around my ears. It was at this very instant that I realized that this was the nasty Saturday night fighter that I had wanted to avoid. His name was Bob Boardman.

From that time forward we gradually became friends. We worked very hard to become the best Marines we could be and in the process teamed up with a great group of guys who pretty much stuck together for the entire war.

Bob and I began to spend most of our free time together and became best friends. We went on many adventurous and sometimes hair-raising liberties together, the last of which put

*Bob in the hospital and completely turned his life around. I
shudder when I think about what might have happened had
he not ended up in the hospital that night. The word Brig
comes to mind most often.*

In Australia as replacements, D.I. Bahde and I managed to be
assigned to the same tank. We went through the battle of Cape
Gloucester, New Britain. After Gloucester and Peleliu, D.I. was a sergeant tank commander in the battle of Okinawa, where he distinguished himself many times in heavy fighting. He describes the
fanaticism of the Japanese:

*My crew and I were out scouting for targets one day when we
came around a corner in the road and about 75 yards ahead
of us were about 50 Japanese soldiers. One of these soldiers
came charging our tank on foot and I noticed that he had
something large taped to his chest. He was carrying heavy
explosives and was going to sacrifice his life by running into
my tank and disabling it. Then the rest of the soldiers would
swarm our tank and kill us all. Fortunately my gunner was
able to shoot him with our 75mm cannon. The explosion of
our shell and his explosives was tremendous. Smoke finally
cleared and the rest of the soldiers had disappeared into
caves. We survived another day.*

In another incident on Okinawa, over very difficult terrain, an
enemy emplacement D.I.'s tank was trying to destroy had pinned
down the accompanying infantry.

D.I. observed two seriously wounded infantrymen unable to move
in the path of his tank. Without hesitation, he promptly dismounted
and in the face of concentrated enemy fire, crawled to these wounded
men and carried them one by one to the safety of his vehicle. For this
and other actions he received the Silver Star citation.

Is there any more valuable earthly treasure than this kind of
camaraderie? I know of none. It certainly is not silver, gold and the
commodities!

Only the riches of personally knowing Jesus Christ as Lord and
Savior and soon returning King and Judge of all the earth can
supersede the above comradeship! In fact, it is the basis of our closest human relationship.

* * *

SCRIPTURE: *I give you a new command, to love one another. Just as I have loved you, you too must love one another. By this everybody will know that you are my disciples, if you keep showing love for one another.* — John 13.34,35

PRAYER: *Heavenly Father, especially give me love for those I can't even like. Only You can do this. Let the love of Christ motivate me and overflow to the humanly unlovable. Amen.*

* * *

THE SECRETARY OF THE NAVY
WASHINGTON

The President of the United States takes pleasure in presenting the SILVER STAR MEDAL to SERGEANT DONALD I. BAHDE, UNITED STATES MARINE CORPS RESERVE, for service as set forth in the following CITATION:

"For conspicuous gallantry and intrepidity while serving as a Tank Commander of the First Tank Battalion, First Marine Division, in action against enemy Japanese forces on Okinawa, Ryukyu Islands, 22 May 1945. During an assault over difficult terrain, Sergeant Bahde was attempting to move his tank forward and destroy an enemy emplacement which had pinned down the accompanying infantry, lying in the path of his tank and unable to move, he promptly dismounted from his tank in the face of concentrated enemy fire and, crawling to the wounded men, carried them, one at a time, to the safety of his vehicle. Thereafter, he continued to advance and carry out his mission of destroying the enemy fortifications. His initiative, coolness under fire and unselfish devotion to duty were in keeping with the highest traditions of the United States Naval Service."

— John L. Sullivan,
Secretary of the Navy for the President

Capt. Geoff Gorsuch,
USAF, Vietnam, 1972.

Geoff is Navigator staff today living in
the Denver, Colorado area.

Nine

A MOMENT OF TRUTH

By Geoff Gorsuch

OH LORD! Thou knowest how busy I must be this day: if I forget Thee, do not forget me. March on boys!
> — Sir Jacob Hill, 23 October 1642, before battle during the
> English Civil War.

"SAM! SAM! SAM!" the radios squawked.

A Surface to Air Missile (SAM) was on the hunt. Warnings screamed continuously in my earphones as enemy radar frequencies shifted from a "searching" mode to "tracking." The "red light" flashing on my instrument panel told me I had about ten seconds to execute countermeasures and evade it. But before I could do any of that...I had to see it!

Bill, my navigator, screamed at me over the "hot" intercom, "I see it...I see it...nine o'clock low." Sweat burst from every pore as my eyes searched the treetops below.

"Where?" I said, my head on a swivel, "I can't see it!"

"Below and behind us now!" he yelled, unconscious of his fear-filled volume. "Bank hard right...further...further...there! See it?"

"No joy!" I said as I yanked us into a steep diving turn. "I got it!" I got it!" Belching out a telltale trail of white smoke, the missile was closing fast. Too fast!

"Jesus!" I heard Bill sigh, "Save us."

A few seconds later, the "moment of truth" had come: the defining moment in the life of a combat pilot—the moment when you have only a two-second window to escape certain death! A point in time and space when the missile is too close to correct on your final evasive maneuver, but not yet close enough to detonate. The moment when your life and someone else's depends entirely on your next move. Break too soon and the missile can still track you. Break too late...

"...Now!" I shouted to myself as I slammed the thrust levers into the firewall. I rolled right into the missile's trajectory—"playing chicken" with death. But, just before the missile exploded, I rolled the aircraft inverted and yanked it down and away, hoping against hope that the hundred or so feet that now separated us would also cushion the plane from the deadly blast. There was nothing more I could do.

We held our breath...

Memories flooded my mind with the force of a tsunami: a middle-class family, loving parents, Christmas trees, a church, my two brothers, high school basketball, the Air Force Academy, pilot training, receiving orders and, finally, arriving in a war zone.

Then...a flash of light!

The reality of war: a muffled roar, the ping of the shrapnel, a shock wave, the plane out of control, a death grip on the stick, the altimeter unwinding, death lingering over us and the earth rising too fast beneath us. And, above it all the cry of the man behind me, "Jeeesus...save us!"

Fly the plane, I thought, *fly the plane!*

I quickly read the instruments as I wrestled with the "sloppy stick." *Tail damage!* But, after a couple of seconds, I realized the blast had not been fatal. This bird was still alive…and so were we! I kicked the rudder hard to stop the death spiral. Then I pulled back on the stick…and prayed the tail could still sustain the g-forces!

"C'mon…c'mon…fly," I whispered to God under my oxygen mask as the craft shuddered on the edge of a stall. Another second passed…then…another…finally, the altimeter stopped. A moment later it started to climb. As I looked outside, we surged through the horizon and shot upward! And a quick glance back inside revealed that all instruments were miraculously "in the green." *We just might make it!* I thought.

But, before I could say it, Bill burst out, "Wow! What a piece of flying. I can't believe it…" And he went on letting it all out…until he finally whispered thanks to the One who really deserved it.

We'd made it!

About twenty minutes later, safely on the ground, we examined the shot-up tail assembly. Our knees buckled! That's when we knew we were no longer the same. There had been some "collateral damage." That normally occurs when there are unforeseen negative results in a mission: a "guided" bomb goes astray or there's "pilot error," causing innocent lives to suffer. But our collateral damage was different. We had clearly "dodged a bullet." A big one! But after the debriefing, our hearts sank. We couldn't evade the psychological aftermath of war. We were overwhelmed with "what's the use!" Darkness!

We were now "old heads." In just a few minutes of kill-or-be-killed combat, we had aged a couple of decades. We could no longer tell ourselves that we were "in control" or that our generation would slay the dragons and never get hurt. Youthful dreams of a better world had been smashed on the rocks of reality. Our innocence was gone. We had discovered—in an unforgettable way—our own mortality. We, too, would die! And we were still too young to know that…still too young to handle the pain. And the world's painkillers were at our fingertips, offered by a war zone black market catering to the flesh.

But we remembered! Earlier in the day when the "moment of truth" had come, each of us had cried out to God! In the madness that ensued, more than just professional training had brought us home. God did. But having been "kissed by death," we were now facing another moment of truth in a different war—the war for our souls. Would we let the psychological pain drive us into the painkillers and turn us into cynics, or would our pain become our rendezvous with God, as the Bible had promised?

We had a choice to make. As we once again asked for the help that only God could give, we looked into our Bibles and read:

> *How can you say that the Lord does not see your troubles…He gives power to those who are tired and worn out; He offers strength to the weak. Even youths will become exhausted and young men will give up. But they that wait upon the Lord will find new strength. They will fly high on wings like eagles. They will run and not grow weary. They will walk and not faint. —Isaiah 40.20*

That night, we chose to wait upon God.

The next day, the promise proved true! In spite of the overwhelming feelings of discouragement the night before, as the sun rose, so did our spirits. The experience of having given our troubles to God had allowed us to rise "on eagle's wings." We had broken through. Through pain, two men had moved beyond the deadening routine of religion and into the power of a personal relationship with God. Faced with the physical and spiritual realities of war, God had proven Himself faithful…on both fronts!

And it's been that way ever since.

☆　　☆　　☆

SCRIPTURE: *The Lord is my light and my salvation: whom shall I fear? The Lord is the strength of my life; of whom shall I be afraid? When the wicked, even my enemies and my foes, came upon me to eat up my flesh, they stumbled and fell. —Psalm 27.1,3*

PRAYER: *Lord, in both my weakness and as I am tempted to fear— no matter what circumstances I am in—may the promises of Your rock-like Word be my hope and my anchor. In Jesus' name. Amen.*

CITATION TO ACCOMPANY THE AWARD OF
THE SILVER STAR
TO GEOFFREY S. GORSUCH
For Gallantry in Action
5 April 1972

Captain Geoffrey S. Gorsuch distinguished himself by gallantry in connection with military operations against an opposing armed force as a Forward Air Controller directing fighter aircraft in Southeast Asia on 5 April 1972. On that date, Captain Gorsuch was engaged in a search and rescue operation when he was fired upon by numerous surface to air missiles launched from North Vietnam. With complete disregard for his own personal safety and regardless of the fact that his aircraft had sustained battle damage, Captain Gorsuch evaded the missiles and intense groundfire to accurately pinpoint the launch site and direct its destruction. By his gallantry and devotion to duty, Captain Gorsuch has reflected a great credit upon himself and the United States Air Force.

John W. Vogt, General,
USAF Commander, Seventh Air Force

Pfc. Boyce Clark, USMCR, and wife Charlotte, 1950, prior to his departure for Korea.

E. Boyce Clark today in Seattle, Washington is active in veteran's affairs.

Ten

THE GOOD LIFE

by Earl Boyce Clark

When he [Tsar Alexander I] reviewed the French Army and at Napoleon's side watched the Old Guard march past, he was struck by the scars and wounds which many of these veterans bore. "And where are the soldiers who have given these wounds?" he exclaimed. "Sire, they are dead."

— Sir Winston Churchill, *The Age of Revolution*, 1957
of the meeting of Napoleon and Alexander I of Russia
at Tipsit, 7-9 July, 1807

I was discharged from the US Marine Corps twice. The first time was 5 January 1948, before reaching my twenty-first birthday. I then joined the "52-20" Club in Seattle. This exclusive club offered each veteran $20 per week for 52 weeks. Much of it my buddies and I spent at Lucky Boy Tavern, where we discussed our futures and plans for the "good life."

Soon funds from the "52-20" Club dried up and I enrolled in Seattle College, now University. Life was good—parties and basketball practice in the fall, and parties and baseball in the spring. But then I dropped out to go to work.

Soon, however, the best thing that ever happened in my life brought real meaning when I persuaded Charlotte Lou Lumbert to become my wife in March 1950. Life was now really good!

We both had had a rather fragmented Christian background. Charlotte was raised in the Lutheran faith and I attended Briscoe Boy's School and then O'Dea High School, both run by the Jesuit Christian Brothers. The Brothers taught us well. I always had a belief in God, or professed being a Christian. But I found out the hard way that "professing" and "being" are two different things.

In June 1950, the good life we enjoyed changed dramatically. War came to far off Korea. Reserve units were frantically called up to serve in what President Harry Truman referred to as a "police action." I assured Charlotte that as an inactive reserve I would not be recalled. Wrong! I came home from work one day and a large manila envelope "invited" me to join with other Marines to take a train ride to Camp Pendleton near Oceanside, California.

Before long, eighteen hundred US Marines boarded ship for a fourteen day "cruise" to Korea and the awaiting "police action." We ended up at Masan in a place they called the Bean Patch. On Christmas Eve 1950, there was a light snow falling and a bunch of us were singing Christmas carols.

For the next six months I served as a Fire Team Leader in Easy Company, Second Battalion, Seventh Marine Regiment, First Marine Division. Our mission was to seek out, attack and destroy enemy elements. I was involved in the Pohang Guerilla Hunt and Operations Killer, Ripper. By February 1951, the weather was really lousy with a mix of wet snow, rain, mud and slush. Everyone was cold to the bone and everything was soaked—clothes, parkas, weapons, rations and ammo.

On 24 February 1951, my twenty-fourth birthday, we fought up hills and ridges against stiffening Chinese resistance. Another memorable date for me was 4 March, our first wedding anniversary. I told my platoon leader, Lieutenant Buttel, that this was one hell of a way to spend my anniversary. He pulled a flask of Canadian VO out of his pack and we toasted Charlotte.

I spoke of being a "professing" Christian. Not a night went by that I did not pray and ask God for His mercy. I would pray that mortar and artillery shelling would not land in our midst and that we would be spared.

As the fighting intensified, I would call upon Him for strength. The strength to climb the next mountain, the strength to confront the enemy and the strength not to let my fellow Marines down. The Lord Jesus Christ answered my prayers. On 6 April 1951, I along with eight other Marines from E-2-7 were wounded during a morning assault. Amazingly, none were killed in this action. My prayers were once again answered, and after a brief stay in a field hospital, I returned to my company.

As June approached, the Seventh Marines, after sixty days on the front lines, were to be relieved by the First Marines, who would pass through our lines and continue the attack. At approximately 0800 on 2 June 1951, a communist mortar barrage landed in our assembly area. The attack came as a complete surprise. The Chinese had the hilltop zeroed in and just kept shelling the area for what seemed an eternity. The shelling probably lasted no more than ten minutes, but the damage had been done. Fragments from a 120mm mortar tore through my left arm, almost severing it at the elbow. Thirty-two other Marines from the First and Seventh Regiments were also wounded at this time.

After being hit, I thought, "The war is over for me, I'll soon be going home." In the meantime, people around me were calling "Corpsman, corpsman," and mortars were still killing and wounding Marines. I did not lose consciousness when wounded. In fact, I took a pack strap and placed it as tight as I could just above my elbow to try to stop the flow of blood. I remember yelling out that I was hit then rolling over and grabbing my arm. It seemed forever, but in no time a corpsman was at my side administering morphine and stabilizing my arm.

As I was being evacuated and carried down the hill, my face was covered by a piece of clothing. Someone asked if it was E.B. and was he dead? I removed the covering and assured him that I was very much alive!

I spent the next couple of days in the hospital, while doctors tried to save my arm. On 5 June, I was transported to the hospital ship USS *Haven*. After all attempts by the doctors and staff, it was decided to amputate the arm just above the elbow.

A Navy chaplain came to my bunk and informed me that the surgery was necessary. He asked if I wanted him to remove my wedding ring and then replace it on my right hand after the surgery. I responded in the affirmative. The chaplain left and said he'd see me in the morning, right after surgery. The chaplain did come back and we talked for quite some time before saying a prayer and placing my wedding ring on the third finger of my right hand. Then it was time to head Stateside.

I was taken to Oak Knoll Naval Hospital in Oakland, CA, where I spent the next several months going through various kinds of physical therapy in order to utilize an artificial arm. The best part of this hospitalization was that "Chauzz," my wife, could be with me.

Finally, on 31 October, I was discharged from the hospital and the US Marine Corps for the second time. I will never forget those fellow Marines and continue to pray for them. A Bible verse from Matthew expresses my feeling: "Well done, good and faithful Servant" (Matthew 25.21).

The Lord has indeed watched over me and continues to do so. There are things I know for certain: the love and respect I have for Charlotte, my wife, lover and very best friend; the immense pride and love I have for my sons Michael and Dennis, and for my lovely daughter Diane. We are blessed with grandchildren Taylor, Spencer, Eilea and Daydra. I am thankful for my loving family, for my service to Country and Corps, and moreover, for a faithful God that continually demonstrates His love for me.

I have discovered over a lifetime that the "good life" only comes with the price of hardships and suffering. And I am grateful to God.

Semper Fidelis,
Earl Boyce Clark, E-2-7
First Marine Division

✯　✯　✯

84

SCRIPTURE: *I beg you, therefore, brothers, through these mercies God has shown you, to make a decisive dedication of your bodies as a living sacrifice, devoted and well-pleasing to God, which is your reasonable service. — Romans 12.1*

PRAYER: *LORD, some of our bodies, like Boyce's, are battered and worn; nevertheless I give mine to You as a living sacrifice to use till the end for Your glory and honor. In Jesus' name. Amen.*

Lt. Doug Mastriano, US
Army, 1991

Major Doug Mastriano, wife Rebecca and son Josiah now stationed in Germany.

⋆ Eleven ⋆

DESERT STORM BRINGS PEACE

by Major Douglas V. Mastriano, USA

Trust is a distinguished reward for warriors.
— SunBin, *The Lost Art of War,* 350 B.C.

My story begins on 9 November 1990, when President George Herbert Walker Bush and then Secretary of Defense Dick Cheney announced that the Second Armored Cavalry Regiment was one of several units designated to leave Germany to deploy to Saudi Arabia. The announcement caught us entirely by surprise. As time went on, the news continually worsened for us. We were told that our time in Saudi Arabia may last beyond a year, and that if war did break out, to expect 70 percent losses in personnel.

Despite this collection of bad news, my wife Rebbie and I felt a deep heart peace that was humanly inexplicable.

My first direct evidence of God's protection occurred shortly after the air war commenced. One night, my driver and I were sleeping in a shallow trench in our perimeter. Since we were at war and not far from Iraqi positions, vehicles operated in "black-out drive," which means that the headlights are off. When you enter a perimeter, the vehicle's passenger must dismount and lead the vehicle through on foot, so no one is accidentally run over. One night the passenger in a vehicle was too lazy and told his driver that he was not going to dismount. As we slept, this vehicle headed directly for our position. The perimeter guard was Corporal Trump, one of the few who knew where my driver and I were sleeping. Trump had a nagging voice inside him that kept telling him to get back inside the perimeter. At first he resisted, since he was on guard duty and certainly must not abandon his post. However, the urgency of the feeling intensified, and he left his post.

As Trump neared the location where my driver and I were, he saw the vehicle heading straight for us. Trump stopped the vehicle only three feet from running over my driver and me. The next morning I awoke to see the evidence of the tire tracks in the sand.

THE GROUND WAR: IRAQI CHEMICALS AND THE PREVAILING WINDS

We had numerous reasons to anticipate Iraqi use of chemical weapons against us. The primary reason for this was the prevailing winds. The wind normally blows from Iraq (northwest) into Saudi Arabia (southeast). This meant that if the Iraqis used chemical weapons, the wind would carry the toxins deep into the American lines. Another reason to believe that Saddam would use chemicals was recent history. Saddam directed extensive use of chemical weapons against the Iranians during the 1980-1988 war against Iran and even ordered a deadly chemical attack against his own Kurdish people in 1988. This, combined with the prevailing winds, convinced us that it was inevitable that we would face a chemical attack.

Evidence of divine intervention was manifest in Southern Iraq at 1330 hours, 23 February 1991. After firing a series of artillery strikes, my regiment crossed the two five-meter-high border berms that separate Iraq and Saudi Arabia. It was G-Day minus one with the ground war to officially commence the next day. Our move into Iraq began the offensive. My regiment was to lead the US Army's VII Armored Corps against Saddam's elite Republican Guards. This was the main effort for the coalition.

The very instant that our tanks entered Iraq, a strange thing occurred. I noticed quite a few little dust devils all around me. The direction of the prevailing winds changed. When our regiment's tanks entered Iraq at 1330 on 23 February, the wind changed from the prevailing course that blew from Iraq into Saudi Arabia to the opposite direction, from Saudi into Iraq. Such an event had severe repercussions on any plans that Saddam had on using tactical chemical munitions. If he used them now, they would blow right back into his own troops. The miraculous thing about this wind is that it generally stayed this way until 0800, 28 February, the very instant of the ceasefire going into effect. This highlights the power of prayer of God's people.

DELIVERANCE FROM CERTAIN DEATH

Another dramatic intervention is more significant to me and my family than all the others mentioned here. I would have been one of them. Before the decisive Battle of 73rd Easting, the Twelfth Iraqi Armored Division moved from its positions near the Iraq-Kuwait-Saudi borders in a northwest direction to block the movement of the US VII Corps. A company-sized element of the Twelfth Iraqi Armored, equipped with tanks and armored personnel carriers, attacked our lightly defended Regimental Support Squadron (RSS). Upon making contact with this Iraqi force, RSS called upon Fourth Squadron for help. Fourth Squadron was the best suited to counter this threat, since we could respond faster than tanks.

When we received the request for assistance, I was in a UH-60 Blackhawk helicopter with the squadron's operations officer, fire support officer and six others. Our available Attack Helicopter Squadron (Quickstrike Troop) was on the ground and needed about five minutes to respond. Since we were already airborne, the operations officer decided that we would head to the location that RSS called for help and make it easier for Quickstrike to find the enemy when they arrived. This was about all we could do since our Blackhawk had only two M-60 machine guns.

There was not a moment to lose. We arrived at the location where the battle occurred but found neither Iraqi nor American vehicles in the area. To locate the enemy vehicles, we slowed our airspeed and increased our flying altitude slightly and continued the search. However, this maneuver made it easier for the Iraqis to engage us. Within an instant, we stumbled right into a group of Iraqi armored vehicles, which immediately engaged us at point blank range. We were literally right on top of them and had not realized it.

I glanced out of the left door gunner's window and saw that we were so close to the enemy I could see fire coming out of their 12.5mm machine guns. Everything began to move in slow motion at this point. It was evident that we might die. I nodded at the operations officer, who alerted the crew, and then abruptly rolled the Blackhawk helicopter down and away from the attack. After we vacated the area, Quickstrike arrived with their AH-1 Attack Cobra helicopters and contended with the adversary. Although it was painfully obvious that there was divine intervention to spare our lives on that day, I did not ponder it much.

However, a few weeks later during an Easter service conducted by our regimental chaplain near the ancient Iraqi town of Ur, the point came home. At the end of the service, the chaplain asked us to stand up and recite the "Soldier's Psalm" (Psalm 91). I figured this was not a problem since we read it so often during the war. However, when we read verses 14 and 15 the Holy Spirit gripped my heart and brought all of the events in the Blackhawk back to mind. *Because he has set his love upon me, therefore will I deliver him. I will set him on high because he has known my name. He shall call upon Me and I will answer him; I will be with him in trouble; I will deliver him and honor him. —Psalm 91.14,15*

The message was clear. The eight other men and I were only alive because of God's grace and intercessory prayers. There was no human reason to have hope or joy in those uncertain times, both before and during the war. Yet it was made very clear that God would take care of us and that this whole situation was in His will. There was no promise of a safe return, except the assurance of Him walking with us through the adversity and uncertainty that lay ahead. It took the turmoil of war for many of us to accept this fact.

✶　✶　✶

SCRIPTURE: *Have I not commanded you? Be strong and of good courage; do not be afraid, nor be dismayed, for the Lord your God is with you wherever you go —Joshua 1.9*

PRAYER: *Lord, You are at work in peacetime and in times of battle and stress. Your sovereign will is being accomplished. Help me, Lord, when I observe Your marvelous works to never be ashamed to proclaim them with great boldness. Amen.*

☆   ☆   ☆

ARMY COMMENDATION MEDAL

For meritorious achievement during Operation Desert Shield and Operation Desert Storm while serving as the Intelligence Officer, Headquarters and Headquarters Troop, Fourth Squadron, 2nd Armored Cavalry Regiment. First Lieutenant Mastriano performed admirably in time of war and never wavered in his patriotism, fidelity and devotion. His ability to quickly decipher reports and correctly determine the enemy size and intent led to successful destruction of the enemy. First Lieutenant Mastriano's extraordinary efforts and accomplishments reflect distinct credit upon him, VII Corps and the United States Army.

28 April 1991
Signed by LTG Frederick Franks, Jr., VII Corps Commander

★ III ★

Man's Extremity Is God's Opportunity

When I lay me down to sleep, I recommend myself to the care of Almighty God; when I awake I give myself up to His direction. Amidst all the evils that threaten me, I will look up to Him for help, and question not but that He will either avert them or turn them to my advantage.

Though I know neither the time nor the place of my death, I am not at all solicitous about it, because I am sure that He knows them both. He will not fail to support and comfort me.

— Admiral Viscount Nelson, 1793

Sgt. Ron York, USMC and
Silver Star, Korea, 1951.

Ron and Joyce York today in Osburn, ID. They are Navigator staff.

Twelve

SERGEANT YORK LIVES AGAIN... AND AGAIN

Sergeant York of A-1-7

by Bob Boardman

Ron York joined the Marine Corps at age eighteen to seek adventure and to become a real man. He ended up in Korea's "Forgotten War." His journey into manhood changed him in the most unexpected and incredible way.

The famed First Marine Division, which had won three Presidential Unit Citations out of four battles in World War II, was now precariously trapped in the Chosin Reservoir in Korea. The time was between 17 November and 10 December 1950. The outcome was in doubt in the freezing mountainous terrain of North Korea. Surrounded by fourteen divisions of over 110,000 Chinese soldiers, the Division fought a tenacious strategic withdrawal, bringing out all their wounded and dead. In the process the Marines destroyed eight enemy divisions and won yet another Presidential Unit Citation.

The Marine Corps flew hundreds of Marines to Japan as replacements to be trans-shipped to Korea.

PFC Ron York was one of those. After arriving, he was transported to the Naval Base in Yokosuka where he ran into some of the casualties. One Marine on crutches stopped Ron and asked, "How old are you?"

Ron answered, "Eighteen."

The wounded man replied, "Buddy, you'll never see nineteen." Chills ran down York's spine.

In a few days, Ron's replacement draft departed on a small Japanese ship from Sasebo, Japan to Pusan in southern Korea. It was Christmas Eve, 24 December, 1950. Ron described the desolate scene, "We propped up a bedraggled broom, hung some fruit and candy on it and quietly wept as we sang a few carols. Little did I know that I was headed for the most terrifying year of my life."

Ron York was raised in the small mining town of Kellogg, Idaho. He felt secure in his parents' love for him. "The love of fishing and hunting also kept me from many teenage hangups."

Ron continued, "Life's first hard jolt for me came as a senior in high school when my parents divorced. I wanted to escape that world of confusion, so upon graduation, I joined the Marine Corps in 1950. I was also small of stature and skinny and felt the Corps would make a man out of me and bring the respect I longed for."

Don Lewis and Billy Ray, two of Ron's closest high school buddies, were both killed in combat in Korea in a war that claimed 54,246 dead, 103,284 wounded, 8,177 missing and 7,000 POWs.

Upon landing in Pusan, York was integrated into A Company First Battalion Seventh Marine Regiment (A-1-7). They fought from the Pusan Perimeter north to Taegu, then headed north fighting to the "Quantico Line."

On 22 April 1951, the Chinese Communist Forces (CCF) began their spring offensive. York says: "A-1-7 was at the extreme left flank of the Division. Nearly two thousand grenade-throwing, bugle-blowing Chinese swarmed upon us in the dark. I remember our own shells screaming over us. Some landed short into our troops. I can still hear the agonizing cries of dying men."

One by one Ron's comrades in A-1-7 disappeared. Jack died instantly with a bullet to the head. Johnny lost a leg, Red a lung and knee. A young Marine, being carried in front of Ron, was praying the Lord's Prayer. "It was all so hard. A thousand times, pictures have flashed by as clear today as fifty years ago," York says.

By June 1951 York was a corporal and carried the Browning automatic rifle in his fire team, led by Floyd Swift. York was decorated with the Silver Star after his platoon was subjected to a vicious hail of automatic weapons, grenades and small arms fire deep in enemy territory.

His citation read:

"On June 11, 1951, when his platoon was conducting a reconnaissance patrol near Imdang-ni, Korea, it was suddenly subjected to a vicious hail of automatic weapons, grenades and small arms fire from a well emplaced and numerically superior enemy force. Although deep in enemy territory and under intense fire, Cpl. York skillfully maneuvered his fire team into a position from which he could bring fire to bear on the fanatical enemy and thus relieve some of the pressure on the remainder of his platoon which was pinned down.

"During the ensuing action Cpl. York's position was subjected to attack, and although painfully wounded during this action by an enemy hand grenade, he rallied his men and without regard for his own personal safety remained in an exposed position directing the fire in such a highly efficient and well coordinated manner that the attack was repulsed. It was only after the successful repulse of the enemy attack and the integrity of his position assured that Cpl. York, who by this time was greatly weakened from loss of blood from his wound, consented to be evacuated.

"His heroic actions and self sacrificing devotion to duty were a material factor in contributing to the success of his platoon's mission and served as an inspiration to all who observed him."

Signed: Secretary of the Navy
John A. Kimball

After hospitalization York returned to A-1-7. The name York sometimes evoked comments like: "Any relation to Sergeant York of WW1 Fame?"

"No, but he's always been a hero of mine," York would reply.

All was not well back on the home front. Ron's forty-eight-year-old father turned to alcohol after his divorce. One night in a horrible car accident, his back was broken. In the hospital someone gave him a Bible. As he read, Ron's dad decided that Jesus Christ could fill the vacuum in his life. Ron said, "Now in his letters to me he began to tell me about those changes. He would insert Bible verses for me to read, so I picked up a Gideon New Testament from the chaplain."

Ron continued, "I soon learned that the penalty of sin is death and if I were to die I would likely go to hell. Dad continued to tell me how Christ had died for my sins and rose again from the dead. If I would believe in Him as my Savior and follow Him, He would give me a new life and hope. In August 1951 I said 'Yes' to God and accepted Christ."

Ron York found temporal fulfillment and respect in the Marine Corps, but deep inner fulfillment and eternal peace in Jesus Christ.

...AND AGAIN

Over fifty years after Ron York's dramatic and heroic experience in the Korean War, he again came very close to losing his life in Alaska. In those interim fifty years, Ron lost his first wife to cancer, served faithfully as a missionary with his second wife, Joyce, to the people of Korea, Japan, the Philippines, Thailand and Alaska.

On Father's Day, 17 June 2001, at age sixty-nine, Ron and two friends who were guests at his Classic View Lodge near Wasilla, Alaska, were fishing. At the confluence of Peter's Creek and the Kahiltna River, Ron fell down a fifty-foot embankment into the ice cold waters and was being swept along toward certain death with a broken neck:

I was knocked unconscious as I fell down the cliff, but miracu-
lously regained consciousness when I hit Peter's Creek. I tried to
swim but my arms and legs were paralyzed. Another miracle
was the absence of any fear and the wisdom to hold my breath.

The last downstream fisherman of six wading in the creek spotted Ron's body, caught him and pulled him to shore, saving him from being swept into the fast-moving oblivion of the Kahiltna.

My neck was broken during the fall down the cliff, pinching my
spinal cord, causing paralysis. If I had not held my breath I
would have gotten water in my lungs. Most likely they then
would have attempted CPR on me, but with a broken neck that
could have caused permanent damage to my spinal cord.

Ron was airlifted to Providence Hospital in Anchorage, where he was operated on and the first four vertebrae in his neck were fused. These are the same broken vertebrae that brought permanent paralysis to actor Christopher Reeves.

When the surgeon asked Ron what had happened, Ron answered, "I fell off a fifty-foot cliff."

The doctor replied in wonderment at his survival, "There was some kind of force at work there."

Joyce, standing by the bed, said: "It was our Sovereign God who loves us more than we love ourselves."

Today Ron and Joyce, living in Osburn, Idaho, near where Ron was born, continue their faithful and fruitful service to their Lord and Savior. The only physical aftereffect is limited mobility in turning his head.

It is crystal clear, like handwriting on the wall, that God is not yet finished with Sergeant York's life and ministry. After this last traumatic experience, Ron testifies:

I revel in the knowledge that God threads the needle in life.
With all life's twists and turns, He makes no mistakes. He is
absolutely faithful and we live in complete assurance of His love
for us. We can totally rest our past, present and future with
Him.

All of the above is evidence that the best title for this story is: Sergeant York Lives Again and Again.

***

SCRIPTURE: *The steps of a good man are ordered by the Lord, and he delights in his way. Though he fall, he shall not be utterly cast down: for the Lord upholds him with His hand. — Psalm 37.23,24*

PRAYER: *Thank You, Lord for Your protection from the enemy and from overwhelming circumstances. With You, there are no "accidents." Amen.*

Cpl. Jesse Miller,
US Army Air Corps,
1941

Jesse Miller,
now deceased

Thirteen

JESSE MILLER AND THE BATAAN DEATH MARCH

by Bob Boardman

JESSE MILLER, 1920-2001

He being dead yet speaks.

In the fall of 1940, Jesse Miller, one year out of high school, went to the Navy recruiting office in Casper, Wyoming to enlist. The recruiter looked in his mouth and rejected him outright. "Too many cavities," he said. However, down the hall, the Army Air Corps recruiter grabbed Jesse like a special leftover and signed him right up!

Shortly after basic training, the Eleventh Recruit Squadron was ordered overseas. The troop ship, following a circuitous route, eventually arrived in Manila, the Philippines. Dressed in winter wool uniforms, the men marched eight sweltering, thirsty tropical miles to Nichols Air Field, which today is Manila International Airport. Soon they were transferred to Clark Air Field, sixty miles north of Manila, and were assigned to the Twentieth Pursuit Squadron.

Jesse Miller had never been away from home before and became desperately lonely and homesick. He says:

I wondered if God truly knew where I was. I felt as though my life was insignificant. Did God care? Like Israel I complained. I did not have my mind fixed on God. But I would learn. God would teach me and would make known His love and His care for me in my environment and through future events through which He would lead me. *

Within eight hours of the Japanese sneak attack on Pearl Harbor, Hawaii, on 7 December 1941, (US time) the enemy also bombed Clark Field. The bases in the Philippines were the closest American installations to Japan so Jesse and his fellow servicemen were prime targets. Jesse had several narrow escapes from death, as most buildings and airplanes were completely destroyed.

God led me out of my self-appointed place of security, into His place of security. He was teaching me to trust Him and obey His WORD. I found fellowship with my Lord there in the midst of great danger, learning that He could take care of me better than I could care for myself. *

Sixteen days after the initial Japanese attack, the American troops in and around Manila and also from Clark Field were evacuated at night by truck convoy onto Bataan Peninsula. They were defeated soldiers before even entering battle and endured the greatest humiliation of any American troops in history.

Initially in the fight on Bataan, morale was high with the constant rumor that help and reinforcements were on the way from America. This was a temporal illusion that quickly turned to despair as slow starvation set in. Reports circulated that the American and Philippine soldiers faced 200,000 well-equipped Japanese regular troops. Surrender took place on 9 April 1942. The horrors of the Bataan Death March were now pending.

The length of the Bataan Death March varied depending on where the marchers started from, but for Jesse Miller it was about seventy-five tortuous miles. Jesse estimated that 8,000 to 12,000 Americans and perhaps 50,000 Filipino troops made the march. Jesse tells the beginning of the agony that took untold thousands of lives under the inhumane treatment from their Japanese captors:

It was frustrating for the enemy to organize us. We were more in number than they expected. There was much confusion with incoming enemy tanks, trucks and artillery to be used in the coming battle against Corregidor. This heavy equipment stirred up horrendous clouds of dust. It was terribly hot and breathing was difficult. The Japanese were shouting orders to us—orders which we could not understand. Their frustrations were vented by slapping and kicking anyone who came in their way. There was no end to the humiliation they wreaked on us. We were at their mercy. The beginning stage of the march claimed the lives of some who were in extremely poor physical condition.

We were lined up and stripped of any earthly possession we had tried to save—our outer clothing, our shoes, watches, rings, billfolds and pictures. If a ring was hard to slip off a finger easily, the finger was cut off. This happened often. Seeing this I quickly took off the Black Hills gold nugget ring which had belonged to my dad. Mom had treasured it and had been hesitant to give it to me. I promised not to lose it. I could not keep that promise.

We were told to lay our possessions on the ground in front of us, and to stand at attention. Out of the corner of my eye I could see what was happening to others. I had a can of milk in that small pile in front of me. I had been saving it for an emergency. I now thought this must be that emergency. Somehow I got that can open and drank that milk without being noticed. At least I thought so.

But my captor saw me! He sneered into my face. Standing at attention, I tried to look past him but noticed the movement of his cheeks and soon felt the wad of spittle he blasted into my face. It was awful! A bitter, bitter experience for me.

I stood, almost naked, and greatly humiliated. Everything was taken from me, even my own dignity.

My pride flared up in anger. I wanted to strike him. I reasoned that I was bigger than he and given the chance I could whip him, even though I was in a very weakened physical condition. But his bayonet spoke loudly. We had already learned the power of the bayonet.

I continued to stand at attention with bitterness welling up and festering in my thoughts. God controlled my actions by bringing into my mind the thought that Christ had been spit upon when He gave His life for me. I saw it all plainly. He took far more rough treatment than I was getting. And He did it for me. I saw anew the Lord Jesus going to the cross of Calvary, being stripped and scourged and spat upon. I understood more clearly the humiliation my Lord experienced for me. *

"Consider Him that endured…lest you be wearied and faint in your minds." – Hebrews 12.4

The order to march was given. Defeated, beaten, exhausted, sick, thirsty, hungry, discouraged, we stepped out on that horrible death march. April is the hottest month in the Philippines where every month is hot. The hot sun drained our energy. I longed, oh how I longed for a drink of cold water. *

Despite the suffering and hardships of the battle of Bataan, the night before the surrender, Miller gathered and led thirteen men in a Bible study. Each man, including Jesse, fought against bitterness at the thought of being abandoned. That final night, nine of these men made life-changing decisions to place their trust in Jesus Christ as their Lord and Savior. Only Jesse and one other survived the Death March, which began the next day. However, even that one man did not survive the hell of prison camp.

In the first six weeks of imprisonment at Camp O'Donnell, a death camp, 2,300 Americans died of starvation, thirst, torture and mistreatment.

At Camp Cabanatuan, another prison camp where Jesse and many others were marched from Camp O'Donnell, a great crisis arose when a prisoner was reported to have escaped. Because of severe mistreatment, there were incidents of desperate attempted escape. The odds of reaching freedom were almost impossible against success.

In some areas surrounding the camp, there were three successive fences of barbed wire eight feet tall. Every prisoner was assigned to a ten-man squad. In Jesse's barracks there were ten squads totaling one hundred men. If one man escaped, or tried to escape, all nine others in the squad were to be shot.

One night at roll call one man was missing from Jesse's group. The remaining nine were ordered to prepare to face the firing squad the next morning. The violence of the volley of bullets slamming into frail and undernourished bodies and the darkness of the path of unknowable death filled the hearts of these nine with great apprehension. Would their loved ones back in the homeland ever find out what really happened at the violent end of their miserable imprisonment?

Jesse kneeled in desperate prayer. He gave himself and his comrades anew into the merciful hands of the Living God. He said:

Immediately I knew there would be no massacre. As determined as our captors were to squeeze the triggers, they could not. It was God who would intervene. There would be no slaughter, I strongly felt. The enemy officer commanded us to return to our barracks and ordered us to be prepared for the shooting the next morning. That evening I witnessed personally to every man in squad nine of Christ's substitutionary death for them. Each man was left with his own thoughts.

The next morning there was no firing line to face. We were ordered back to work; most of us went back to slave labor in the fields and others to their work on airfield construction for the enemy. As I thought of the miracle that had taken place, I realized it was God's mercy which had kept us and delivered us again. *

Jesse was eventually shipped to Japan aboard an infamous "hell ship." Many of these vessels were sunk by American subs because they were unmarked as POW ships. He served as a slave-laborer in Japanese coal mines until the Japanese surrender on 21 September 1945. Three and a half years of malnutrition, disease and hard labor in coal mines finally came to an end.

Five years to the day that he sailed to the Philippines, Jesse passed under the Golden Gate on his return to the Land of the Free and Home of the Brave. It is difficult to summarize Jesse Miller's amazing life and experiences. His own words do it best:

That march seemed to last an eternity. Many delays made it so long for me…standing in line for two or three hours, waiting for the order to move again. For many it was the march of death. But not for me. I had God's Presence with me, and it became a march of faith, trusting Him with every detail of my life. I have often said that I would rather be on that death march today knowing I was in God's will, than to be in America with every comfort, but not knowing I was in His will. The sense of His presence with me was so real! It was most precious. *

Truly man's extremity is God's opportunity.

☆   ☆   ☆

SCRIPTURE: *They were stoned to death, they were tortured to death, they were sawn in two, they were killed with the sword…Men* *of whom the world was not worthy...though all these people by their faith won God's approval... — Hebrews 11.36-39*

PRAYER: *Lord God, give me the kind of faith embodied in Jesse, that when washed in the waters of affliction will not shrink. For Jesus' sake. Amen.*

* All quotes are from Jesse's book, Prisoner of Hope, available from Cadence, PO Box 1268, Englewood, CO 80150.

Fourteen

A MARINE CALLED LITTLE JESUS

by Bob Boardman

I shall tell you a secret my friend. Do not wait for the last judgment. It takes place every day.

— Albert Camus

At some point in Charles G. Meints' Marine Corps career, perhaps when he became a battalion commander, he began to call himself "Little Jesus." I greatly suspect that it related to occasions when he presided over court-martial proceedings when Marines were tried and sentenced for various misdemeanors and crimes.

Throughout the First Tank Battalion he was notorious for his favorite saying, *"Jesus gives and Jesus takes. I am Little Jesus!"* This proclamation put a certain fear, not necessarily religious, into the ranks. No one wanted to incur the wrath and sentencing whims of this kind of commanding officer. I personally would undergo this officer's fearful process in Ballarat, Australia. It would help make me into a man and a Marine.

Charles Meints had been part of the somewhat chaotic formation and early growth of Marine Corps tanks. Before tank battalions were formed, as a captain, he commanded the First Tank Company in the late 1930s.

Then as a major, he took command of First Tank Battalion as it was formed from separate tank companies that existed. Finally in 1942, he was promoted to lieutenant colonel and led the battalion before the battle of Guadalcanal.

After the 'Canal, in which the First Marine Division—which included elements of the First Tank Battalion, the Second Marine Division and the US Army's 164th Regiment—halted the southeast drive of the Japanese Imperial Forces, the division was shipped to Australia.

Victory for the Marines on Guadalcanal and for the Navy in surrounding waters was a crucial turning point in WWII. Before that, Japan, along with its Axis partners, Germany and Italy, were aggressively on their way to conquering the world.

In Ballarat, Australia, a peaceful town before the US Marines arrived, it was my well-deserved fate to come face-to-face with Little Jesus. Even though it was August, Australia's dead of winter, I was sweating out this dreaded encounter.

After tank training at Jaques Farm in San Diego, we were among two thousand Marines in the Seventeenth Replacement Battalion integrated into various units of the depleted First Marine Division in July 1943. We were mostly teenagers—the Japanese literal translation is *greenagers*. We were green, newly cut lumber that needed processing and maturing. Little Jesus would contribute to our matriculation in becoming usable building material.

After a pub crawl in Ballarat most of one afternoon, D.I. Bahde and I were ready to take on the entire Australian Armed Forces. As a result of a brawl, I severed the tendons in my right wrist by missing my opponent and punching out a large plate glass window in a butcher shop.

I spent about two weeks in Australian Military Hospital #88, which caused me to begin seeking the real Jesus, Jesus Christ. But first I had to meet Little Jesus. I thought deeply about my obvious wrongdoings, not only in Ballarat, but also in my short lifespan. I looked back and saw a series of sowing and reaping. Each time was more serious and painful, climaxed by this Ballarat experience.

Released from the hospital, I returned to C Company First Tank Battalion. Soon I was ordered by my company commander to report to Lieutenant Colonel Meints at Battalion Headquarters. Thankfully, it was not for a court-martial, but rather "Office Hours." C Company First Sergeant Payne, a lean, rather dour, no-nonsense career Marine escorted me.

My girlfriend back in Salem, Oregon had given me two religious medallions for protection when I left for war. As I entered the battalion tent and came before Lieutenant Colonel Meints, I clutched these in my left hand, hoping for good luck.

First Sergeant Payne, in a loud, formal voice, read the charges as the Battalion C.O. coldly eyed me sitting in his judgment seat. As a lowly Marine private, I could only haltingly admit, "Sir, guilty as charged." I anxiously awaited my sentence. Little Jesus took his time as he lectured me.

He then intoned my sentence: "Private Boardman, I hereby sentence you to personally apologize to the shopkeeper, pay him for a new window, plus thirty days restriction to camp. A temporary slip with this penalty will be placed in your Record Book. At the end of six months it will be removed if there are no further infractions. Is all this clearly understood?"

"Yes, sir," I replied.

"Dismissed!"

My encounter with Little Jesus was vital in helping me face my wrongdoings and seeing clearly the unchanging law that I reap whatever I sow.

As I carried out my sentence, I realized that Little Jesus had been more than fair. Although he adopted his nickname capriciously, it seems that he may have recognized that even in the misuse of the name of Jesus there is power and that Jesus is the ultimate Judge of heaven and earth.

★★★

SCRIPTURE: *Do not be deceived any more; God is not to be scoffed at. A person will reap just what he sows, whatever it is. — Galatians 6.7*

PRAYER: *Living Lord, search my heart and know me and see if there is any wicked way in me and guide me in Your ancient ways. For Jesus' sake. Amen.*

Lt. Fred Wevodau,
USAF & C7A Caribou,
Vietnam, 1970

Fred Wevodau today in Colorado.,
serving as Navigator staff.

Fifteen

COME HOME TO PAPA

by Fred Wevodau

*War involves in its progress such a train of unforeseen and
unsupported circumstances that no human wisdom can cal-
culate the end.*

— T. Paine

On the broad scale of events in the Vietnam War, 1970 was not a
particularly significant year, at least not to the politicians who
dictated war policy from the sidelines. But to those of us who regu-
larly strapped ourselves to an airplane, each day had its special life and
death realities. For a rookie pilot, flying tactical resupply for the US
Special Forces from the Mekong Delta to the Central Highlands, terrain and weather were every bit the lethal threat that enemy fire was.

My aircraft, the C7A Caribou, was slow and ugly by any standard, but perfectly designed for operating in the forward combat locations of the jungles of Vietnam. Built by DeHavilland of Canada, the Caribou had established its reputation for effectiveness from the bush country of the Canadian north to the outback of Australia. As a young lieutenant it was the perfect opportunity to get my own airplane and truly learn to fly by the seat of my pants, but our mission was not all a "wild west adventure" without its sobering realities. Just a few months earlier, our Phu Cat squadrons had lost three airplanes in just one week of flying in support of a Special Forces camp in the tri-border area of Cambodia, Laos and South Vietnam. The first loss included Chuck, my roommate and friend from our days as student pilots, who was shot down on a mission to airdrop essential ammunition and supplies by our Army comrades under heavy siege in their frontier compound. I can't describe in words the personal trauma and vacuum in my life of losing the camaraderie of Chuck.

Life goes on in war and two months later that painful loss wasn't at the front of my mind as I taxied for takeoff. I was scheduled on an interesting but routine mission to drop a team of insurgents at Quang Tri field, our closest army airstrip to the DMZ, the faint blue line drawn on our maps separating North and South Vietnam. The twenty-five guys in the back of my Caribou were a mixed lot of mercenaries from Cambodia, Laos and other war-ravaged areas. Some of these were the kind of unsmiling guys who would pull the pins on a few hand grenades and secure the release levers with a rubber band so they would be ready to respond in a fraction of a second. The only reason they worked for us was because we gave them more rice than the bad guys did. That night under cover of darkness they would cross the border into North Vietnam on their assigned mission of interdiction and reconnaissance.

Soon my attention was refocused from their role to mine as a rapidly deteriorating series of events made it more and more questionable if any of us would see Quang Tri that day. On the initial ground checks of our navigational equipment, we were unable to get a good lock-on of our TACAN (tactical air navigation) and DME (distance measuring equipment). Given the distance we were from the Da Nang transmitters, that occasionally happened. Besides, we would be under constant radar control as we progressed north to Hue and Quang Tri, or so we thought.

Winter is monsoon season in Southeast Asia and this day we were basically flying underwater. Shortly after leveling off at 10,000 feet I was given a heading out over the South China Sea to avoid a line of especially vicious thunderstorms to the north. Under such conditions it is affirming to have a set of eyes on the ground that see you and the hazards ahead, but it can create a false sense of security. Besides, I was a veteran of over a thousand combat sorties by then and slated for my return to the States before long.

The radio crackled faintly to life, "Radar contact lost, turn left heading 330_ and contact Hue radar on 320.5." I acknowledged and my copilot changed the radio channel only to be greeted by static. By then we had confirmed that our TACAN was indeed inoperative—our first domino to fall in the escalating series of events. I instructed Jerry, my Air Force Academy classmate and copilot, to tune in the ADF at Hue and to also look up the VHF radio channel as a backup for Hue while I went back to Da Nang radar on UHF for an alternate frequency. The ADF is a WWII vintage navigational aid. It will lock onto a local radio station as an aid to fixing aircraft position. We occasionally used it to listen to music on longer, low-pressure hops up the coastline, but it was also known to lock onto a random thunderstorm. In this weather we had no luck with either the ADF or the radios and I was unable to reconnect with Da Nang radar control any longer. A saner estimate of the eroding circumstances would have delayed the mission for another day and turned back south.

Today was increasingly no day for music. Jerry had no experience fine-tuning an ADF, nor for intense instrument flying conditions, as it turned out. I was hard-pressed to do it all myself and in the preoccupation of other cockpit events, suddenly realized that I no longer had enough fuel to get back to Da Nang, even if I could regain use of my radios and navigational aids that were shorting out due to the intense weather.

Suddenly I saw a small break in the clouds and, in the low visibility, spotted the reflection of light off a runway. I pulled off the power and made a steep spiraling descent through that hole, only to discover not a runway, but a long, narrow rice paddy. Those holes in the clouds are called "sucker holes" and with my snap decision I had just played the sucker. Now with mountains to the west and the ocean to the east, we were locked in under a thousand-foot ceiling, easily in the range of even small-arms fire. Because of terrain hazards and increased fuel consumption, I could not climb back into the clouds. Another bad decision had put us one step closer to disaster.

Soon our fuel was below one hundred gallons. We could always ditch on the beach, but the loyalty of our "friends" in the back was moderately suspect. We couldn't even clearly discern if we were in North or South Vietnam. At low altitude, the range of our radios and navigational aids would be drastically reduced, even if we recovered their intermittent use. One option remained.

I had never used the DF (direction finding) steer because I had never needed to. Alternately transmitting on UHF and VHF frequencies, we repeatedly tried to reach Quang Tri tower so they could home in on our radio signal. The silence from our headsets indicated that our options were rapidly approaching zero. Just when it seemed best to give up the quest and head for the coast where we might find a stretch of beach suitable for ditching, a distant voice responded. It was the tower controller at Quang Tri instructing us to depress the mike button and transmit continuously for ten seconds so he could get a fix on us. In return, we received a heading to fly to the Quang Tri airfield that faintly emerged through the heavy rain after a few long minutes. It was like a voice saying, "Come to Papa. Come on home."

Other situations have brought me much closer to death in an airplane. Surprisingly, we never even took enemy fire that day. But this story is more about life than flying. Most of us have made bad decisions and run into unexpected circumstances in our lives. Rarely had I strung poor choices together so effectively to create a recipe for near-disaster like I did that day. Most of life's dark situations take years of "little indiscretions" to create. It is a great comfort to know that regardless of our bad choices and the resulting disorientation, the potential for a life-giving "direction finding steer" is always there. All we need to do is acknowledge the depth of our need, "depress the mike button," and follow the instructions "home to Papa."

Spiritually none of us have the resources to navigate our own way to heaven. Progressive bad choices cause us to end up far off course and the events of our lives begin to reflect that. Life may not yet look like a crash and burn, but you know that things are out of control. You are alone and out of touch with God.

Make that radio call for help. It may be to a friend who is a genuine follower of Christ. It may be to a church that you know has an authentic message of faith. You may actually know the Bible well enough to open it for yourself and hear God's voice leading you back to Himself. For many people it is not a need to know more, but to humble themselves and act on what they already know to be true.

When I turned my aircraft to follow the course given to me by that Quang Tri tower operator, my life was in his hands. I had never met him before. I could not see him. I couldn't see where he was taking me. It was all by faith—just like most of the important things in life. If you have let bad choices put you into a precarious life situation, either now or eternally, hope is only a "radio call" away. Press the mike button and "come home to Papa."

SCRIPTURE: *You will go on crying to Me and making prayer to Me, and I will give ear to you. And you will be searching for Me and I will be there, when you have gone after Me with all your heart. — Jeremiah 29.12,13*

PRAYER: *Lord, when my snap decisions sometimes take me into "sucker holes," and I find myself off course; give me grace and faith to depress the mike button and follow Your instructions to "come on home." — Amen.*

CITATION TO ACCOMPANY THE AWARD OF
THE DISTINGUISHED FLYING CROSS
TO
FRED H. WEVODAU, JR.

First Lieutenant Fred H. Wevodau, Jr. distinguished himself by extraordinary achievement while participating in aerial flight as Co-Pilot of a C-7A aircraft near the Special Forces Camp at Dak Pek, Republic of Vietnam, on 30 May 1970. On that date Lieutenant Wevodau volunteered to fly a combat essential shipment of needed food and supplies into the high threat area surrounding the imperiled camp. As Co-Pilot, he was directly responsible for maintaining communications with the forward air controller and fighter aircraft, the numerous artillery sites along the route of flight and the camp itself, as well as supervising checklist procedures. Despite the hazardous environment created by the surrounding hostile forces and marginal weather conditions, Lieutenant Wevodau was able to maintain the high degree of precision and discipline necessary to accomplish the resupply mission. His courage and professionalism contributed immeasurably to the successful defense of the camp. The professional competence, aerial skill, and devotion to duty displayed by Lieutenant Wevodau reflect great credit upon himself and the United States Air Force.

Secretary of the United States Air Force
Robert C. Seamans

LtCol. Walter "MuMu" Moore, USMC, Vietnam, C.O. 2nd Bn. 5th Regiment 1967

Marines of
2/5 after
fire-fight
Vietnam

Frank and Sally Reasoner wedding 28 December 1962

Camp of 3rd Marine Recon Battalion, Vietnam, named in honor of Lt. Frank Reasoner, MOH

Corporal Tony Smolich USMC, C Co. 1st Tank Battalion, Camp Seymour, Australia 1943

Pop Sims, Orville Finley, TX, Jerry Atkinson, TN, C Co. 1st Tank Battalion salts on Pavuvu before Okinawa

Third Recon. Bn. Marines in Vietnam. Udell Meyers shirtless

USAF Husky helicopter evacuating
casualty in Vietnam

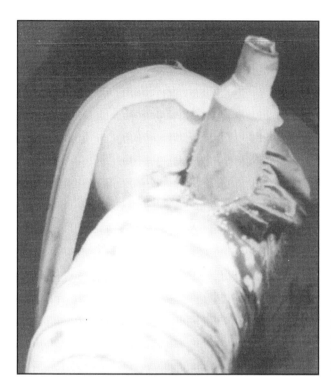

Amputation of
2.75-inch rocket
round tightly
wedged in
Marine's knee

Lieutenant Commander David Taft USN, sitting on burned out Iraqi tank during
Desert Storm, 1991. Note burning oil wells in distance.

Some of the Alphabet Men at Jaques Farm in tank training in 1943. We lived in these eight-man tents. Tough guy with knife is your author. Bud Benkert stands tallest. Others are Brewer, Cornwall and Diedrick.

Boyce Clark, Korea 1951, 7th Marine Regiment

Ron York and Marine patrol Korea, 1950

Recruiter Platoon Sgt. Ron York, USMC, after Korea on recruiting duty in
Coeur d'Alene, Idaho, 1953

Marine Color Guard, Seattle, Platoon Sgt. Ron York, closest one. In old Sick's Stadium Seattle, 1953

Privates Joe Alvarez and Bud Benkert, USMCR, Ballarat, Australia 1943. Both men awarded Silver Star and Purple Heart on Okinawa

Chuck Holsinger's Platoon in the Philippines with captured Japanese battle flags, 1944-45

Chuck Dean, US Army, became a Drill Instructor after Vietnam at Fort Ord, California, 1967-1969

Lt. Jim Horsely's Navy squadron aboard aircraft carrier Midway off Vietnam, 1972

C Company 1st Tank Bn. Mini reunion of Alphabet Men in Colorado Springs, 1958. Standing L to R: Joe Alvarez, Bud Brenkert, Bob Boardman, D.I. Bahde. Kneeling: Bill Henahan and Bill Dunn

The Japanese garrison on Tulagi shortly before the American invasion on August 7, 1942. These men belonged to a crack Special Naval Landing Force. A grim portent of what was to come, they fought to the last man on invasion day. (Photo courtesy of Ted Blahnik)

An armored gun carrier in Korea, 1950

Sketch by Arnie Lyshall

Marines of First Marine Division hitting the beach on Peleliu, 15 September 1944.

First Marine Division landing on Peleliu 15 September 1944.

First Marine Tank Battalion tank/infantry team on Peleliu.

Marines, Corpsmen, and Seabees bringing back casualties from front lines on Peleliu.

Infantry unit moving up to the front on Peleliu.

Peleliu. Sherman Marine tank moving past destroyed Japanese blockhouse.

Marine after 22 straight hours on the front lines crying from exhaustion and shock on Peleliu.

Burial party at sea off of Peleliu.

Sixteen

I WAS A DOG-TAG CHRISTIAN
A WWII Story

by Bob Boardman

Man's Extremity Is God's Opportunity.

When the Japanese Imperial forces attacked Pearl Harbor on 7 December 1941, "a day that will live in infamy," I was a greenhorn youth of seventeen, logging in the woods of eastern Oregon. My life and destiny, as well as that of thousands of other Americans, were changed forever at that crucial, infamous hour.

As the news of the sneak attack filtered through our disbelief and became a reality, many of us immediately quit our jobs and flocked to Navy, Army, Marine Corps and Coast Guard recruiting offices. We flooded there from small towns, farms, ranches, and big cities—all eager for excitement, adventure and retaliation.

Dog-tags? Most of us had never even heard of them. But soon, in boot camp, they would become a significant part of our lives—and the deaths of some of our comrades.

Anyone under eighteen had to have both parents sign papers of releasement to enlist. My mom wouldn't sign so I had to wait about a year. I then chose the Marine Corps. The Corps' exploits in fighting and defeating Japanese aggression and expansion on Guadalcanal in the Solomon Islands attracted and recruited me. The Marines proved themselves a tough, well-trained, well-led fighting force; more than a match for our ruthless enemy.

We recruits traveled south by train heading for boot camp. I can never forget arriving in San Diego well before dawn. It was eerie and depressing. Most major buildings in the city were painted a camouflage design. Large cable-tethered barrage balloons flew over the city to protect against the possibility of bombing and strafing runs by our newly acquired enemy.

The US was on a war footing. Civilians as well as the military were dedicated to achieving the final victory over the Axis Powers, no matter what the cost.

The dog-tags. These were issued to every man upon successfully completing recruit training. The first day in boot camp we were given that special, stylish Marine haircut, dungarees, and certain basic equipment. They also took our blood type, issued each man a serial number and gave us a series of shots. This basic information was then stamped on two metal dog tags which were to be worn around the neck day and night. My serial number was 506095—unforgettable!

These two dog-tags were as much a part of a Marine's career and persona as anything issued in the Corps. The only time they were to be removed was on the occasion of being either wounded in action (WIA) or killed in action (KIA) but we were willing to take our chances in order to serve as Marines.

Another vital piece of information that was stamped on our dog-tags was our religious affiliation. In WWII and the Korean War the designation was simple. If you were a Catholic, C was stamped right after your serial number—or P for Protestant or H for Hebrew. If you were an atheist or agnostic, you drew a blank on your dog-tag. Good luck!

I personally was a P at that time, simply because I wasn't a C or an H. I was a P in name only, stamped on metal.

Shortly before taking that long train ride from Salem, Oregon to San Diego, I was baptized at my parents' earnest request. But this good, traditional sacrament did not change the inside of my heart. My life remained as needy as ever, without inner peace or any type of hope, both in this life and also beyond the grave. If my name and number were to be called by the Grim Reaper, I was not ready to answer. I was only a dog-tag Christian.

After an accelerated wartime boot camp of seven weeks, and after machine gun and tank training, we shipped out to Melbourne, Australia to replace casualties in the First Marine Division of Guadalcanal fame.

As we boarded ship, Red Cross workers gave each Marine a ditty bag of personal items, one of which was a Gideon New Testament. A few weeks later in the little Australian town of Ballarat, while recovering from a severed tendon in my right wrist as a result of a drunken brawl, I began to diligently read that New Testament, seeking for answers.

In its pages I discovered that Jesus Christ loved me so much that He, the Son of God, had been willing to die for all my sins: the fights, excessive drinking, using His name in vain, and all the rest. I learned about His resurrection from the dead, which gave me hope beyond the grave.

On Goodenough Island, near New Guinea in September 1943, I accepted Jesus Christ as my Lord and Savior. He gave my heart the peace that transcends all human understanding. He helped me to move from being a dog-tag Christian—a P stamped on metal—to one upon whose heart Christ's name is stamped forever!

SCRIPTURE: *Then I said, Woe is me! For I am undone; because I am a man of unclean lips, and I dwell in the midst of a people of unclean lips: for my eyes have seen the King, the LORD of Hosts.* —Isaiah 6.5

PRAYER: *Help me to never forget or ever take for granted, LORD, the price You paid through Jesus Christ, to redeem me from my sins. Teach me how to help others who are in a place of extremity. Amen.*

∗ **IV** ∗

Energizing Faith
vs. Unbelief

Soldiers! We have sinned against Almighty God. We have forgotten His signal mercies, have cultivated a revengeful, haughty and boastful spirit. We have not remembered that the defenders of a just cause should be pure in His eyes; that "our times are in His hands"—and we have relied too much on our own arms for the achievement of our independence.

God is our only refuge and our strength. Let us humble ourselves before Him. Let us confess our many sins and beseech Him to give us a higher courage, a purer patriotism and more determined will: that He will convert the hearts of our enemies: that He will hasten the time where war, with its sorrows and sufferings, shall cease, and that He will give us a name and place among the nations of the earth.

— General Robert E. Lee, 13 August 1863,
General Orders 83, Army of Northern Virginia

Seventeen

No Atheists in Foxholes?

by Bob Boardman

In war, many of us become religious. We want to feel closer to God. The ever-present possibility of dying is a constant reminder to put our affairs in order.

— Maj. Gen. Bernard Loeffke

During WWII for over two years and three battles in the Pacific, as the First Marine Division approached their islands of combat, I had seen the desire to become closer to God and to put affairs in order permeate our units. Aboard troop transports and lumbering LSTs, the nearer we came to those islands of destiny and death, the more solemn we became. Divine Services were better attended, also.

Letters written to loved ones back home were part of that solemn process. For a certain percentage of those Marines it would be their last earthly communique. Their final letter would be a priceless, poignant treasure for parents, sweetheart or wife.

Does all this mean then that the popular maxim is true, "There are no atheists in foxholes"? Has all the deep inner reflection and increased attendance at Divine Services—yes, even earnest Bible reading in the lives of men heading for imminent battle—brought about a complete renewal? Has all atheism and agnosticism suddenly fled the combat scene?

In time of war, the general atmosphere of religiousness, seriousness and solemnity increases and certain Marines have, no doubt, had religious conversions, including myself. Two things, perhaps, reveal that for many who turn toward spiritual matters it was an emergency, temporal experience.

First, their dying process on the battlefield reveals that God wasn't an integral part of their life. I have been near or aided men in the battles of Peleliu and Okinawa who have been mortally wounded. Sadly, in several cases, the shock of their fatal or near fatal wounds have brought forth cursing and the name, "Jesus Christ," used in vain.

In contrast, it is interesting that many Japanese wounded and dying repeatedly called out, "Okasan, Okasan!"—"Mother! Mother!" But there were, of course, no loving mothers to answer their pitiful cry.

Secondly, when war is over and survivors return to peacetime pursuits both in the Armed Forces or civilian life, this question of whether our faith is real or not, dogs our steps. Did that pre-battle and battlefield religious experience last and does it make a difference in one's devotion to God and His Son Jesus Christ today? It seems that for some it has lasted, but for others it was only "foxhole religion."

Here is part of an angry letter to a close buddy of mine from a combat Marine that reveals there are, indeed, atheists in those foxholes:

You have apparently made an incorrect assumption that since you have gone religious because of your combat experiences, many of us who experienced similar battle experiences have also done likewise. Nothing could be further from the truth. In fact, looking back, it was those experiences that drove me far afield from any religious affiliation or belief.

I can go even further. I now have completely turned from any thought that there is a god who is loving and merciful. If there were a loving god would he have allowed so many of our buddies to be taken from us and their families in such a violent manner? If there is a god, why does he allow innocent children to be raped, abused and murdered by adults? Yet we are supposed to believe god loves children. What hypocrisy.

I get angrier as I write this. Therefore I will cut it short by asking that you take my name from any lists which are designed to send anything of a religious nature to me.

I will always appreciate hearing from you as a fellow Marine. But only in that vein. Not as a messenger of your religious beliefs.

— Semper Fi, H.A.

God's Word, the Bible, gets right to the heart of the matter when it says in Psalm 14, "The fool [or rebel] has said in his heart, there is no God." This unbelieving attitude is treated in Scripture, not as a sincere, misguided conviction, but rather as an irresponsible gesture of defiance.

The true meaning of this kind of rebellion is self-centeredness, in contrast to a God-centered life. One description of an atheist is *someone with no invisible means of support.*

There can be last-minute hope for the unbeliever, rebel, agnostic or atheist, before the curtain of death opens for that final ride.

At the cross where Jesus Christ, perfect man and perfect God, took our sins upon Him, two criminals were also crucified. One mocked to the end. The other exhibited true repentance. Jesus promised this repentant man the gift of forgiveness and eternal life. This is life's most important choice.

☆ ☆ ☆

SCRIPTURE: *The army captain and his men, who were keeping guard over Jesus [on the cross], who felt the earthquake and saw all that was taking place, were terribly frightened, and said, "Surely this was God's Son." — Matthew 27.54*

PRAYER: *Lord, I Believe! Help me, and cleanse me from any unbelief. Amen.*

Pvt. Joe Alvarez, USMCR, in
Ballarat, Australia, 1943

Joe Alvarez lives today in
San Jose, CA

Eighteen

FATE AND FAITH

The Alphabet Men of C Company
First Tank Battalion

Joe Alvarez's Story

by Bob Boardman

Fate is the same for the man who holds back, the same if he fights hard. We are all held in a single honor, the brave with the weaklings. A man dies still if he has done nothing, as one who has done much.

— Homer in The Iliad, 800 BC

At Camp Elliott in San Diego after boot camp in early 1943, we were "volunteered" alphabetically, A, B, C and D, for Marine Corps tank training at Jaques Farm. The Alphabet Men, of whom I was one, were Alvarez, Atkinson, Aden, Backovich, Bahde, Barwick, Brenkert, Christensen—and many others too numerous to list. Even today, almost sixty years later, I continue to ponder the mysterious fate of being thrown together with some of America's finest, only because of the alphabet.

After Jaques Farm, fate placed us in the Seventeenth Replacement Battalion and we loaded aboard the USS *Rochambeau* in San Diego together with the Eighteenth Replacement Battalion. We made a twenty-eight-day zig-zag "luxury cruise" to Melbourne, Australia. There were 4,000 to 5,000 troops aboard. Down Under we were carefully planted among the depleted ranks of the First Marine Division after the key battle of Guadalcanal.

We were not Marine philosophers, just green, untested-in-combat troops, but our fate continued to carry us together alphabetically, inexorably to close with a no-quarter enemy.

What is *fate*? The dictionary gives fascinating insights: *The cause beyond man's control that is held to determine events: destiny, fortune, disaster, death, outcome.*

There is no doubt in my mind that every living member of the so-called Greatest Generation today still ponders his survival, that of his mates, living and dead, during those crucial and exciting days. I know I do. Was it pure fate that allowed me to become lifelong friends and serve alongside these fellow A, B, C and Ds?

From Jaques Farm on for about two and a half years, until anti-tank, machine gun and sniper fire broke us up in the battle of Okinawa, there were four of us—Alvarez, Bahde, Brenkert and myself—who were as close as brothers through three campaigns. In August 1999, Bud Brenkert took his leave from this earth. On 17 June 1945 over Kunishi Ridge, he and Old Man Christensen rescued me from certain death. I'm forever in their debt.

The second buddy, Joe "Pearls" (the finest set of teeth in the battalion) Alvarez from San Jose, CA, on that same fateful day of 17 June, was at First Tank Battalion headquarters behind Kunishi Ridge. Our battalion commanding officer, Lt. Col. Arthur "Jeb" Stuart, received word by radio that a nearby infantry unit was pinned down and receiving heavy casualties not far from where our own two tanks were knocked out.

Lieutenant Colonel Stuart, in order to make more room, ordered Alvarez to reduce his tank crew of five to two, Joe the commander and his driver, another Alphabet Man, Freeman L. Aden. Aden maneuvered the stripped down tank through the remnants of a sugar cane field, placing it between the enemy and our infantry casualties.

Alvarez dismounted from the gun turret and with complete disregard for his own personal safety, through intense sniper, machine gun and mortar fire, began to hoist wounded infantrymen onto the back of his tank. From the ground he then directed Aden to move the tank in order to pick up more stricken Marines.

In this exposed position Joe was shot in the neck and arm as he courageously lifted a wounded Marine onto his tank. Even after that, he and Aden made several more trips before allowing his own wounds to be treated. Joe's "heroism and devotion to duty were an inspiration to his fellow crewmen." — *from Joe's Silver Star citation.*

Later in the day Joe and I ended up on stretchers side by side holding hands in the well deck of a Navy evacuation barge that took us out to the hospital ship, USS *Solace.* To this day Joe says, "I can never forget the hospital ship's high boom that hoisted us on our stretchers high in the air swaying back and forth and then our being lowered onto the deck. What a terrifying ride!"

Fate is much like that helpless, uncertain, sometimes terrifying ride swaying on a fragile stretcher, high over the Pacific Ocean's fathomless depths. No control. At the mercy of the unknown, unseen operator. Sweating it out. It's easy to become pessimistic, to lose hope, to be as Dryden described:

All things are by fate, but the poor blind man sees but a part of the chain, the nearest link, his eyes not reaching to that equal beam which poises above all.

Epicurus may have said it best: *A strict belief in fate is the worst kind of slavery; on the other hand, there is comfort in the thought that God will be moved by our prayers.*

We are not helpless victims of an unknown power and blind destiny if we exercise energizing faith, as tiny, Jesus said, as a grain of mustard seed. An upturned heart to the living God and His Son Jesus Christ changes a hopeless, pessimistic fate into a living hope. Fate then becomes, not our ruler, but our servant.

Have faith in God — Jesus.

✭ ✭ ✭

SCRIPTURE: *Jesus said, what is the kingdom of God like? And to what shall I compare it? It is like a grain of mustard seed which a man took and sowed in his garden; and it grew and became a tree, and the birds of the air made nests in its branches. — Luke 13.18,19*

PRAYER: *Lord, give me the physical and spiritual courage of Joe Alvarez. Help me to grow from mustard-seed size faith to that of a great tree for Your glory. Amen.*

☆   ☆   ☆

JOSEPH RAMON ALVAREZ'S SILVER STAR CITATION

For conspicuous gallantry and intrepidity in action against the enemy while serving as a gunner with a Marine tank battalion on OKINAWA SHIMA, RYUKYU ISLANDS, on 17 June 1945. While engaged in evacuating wounded Marines from forward of friendly lines to a battalion aid station, Sergeant ALVAREZ voluntarily, and with complete disregard for his own personal safety, rode in a precarious position on the back of his tank giving aid to the wounded men and protecting them with his body. Although wounded while thus exposing himself to enemy machine gun and sniper fire, he made several trips in this manner before having his own wounds treated. His heroism and devotion to duty were an inspiration to his fellow crewmen and were in keeping with the highest traditions of the United States Naval Service.

— Roy S. Geiger
Lieutenant General, US Marine Corps

Sketch by Arnie Lyshall

Bob Boardman in uniform, reunited with Bud Brenkert, 1947.

Nineteen

LEARNING PATIENCE AS A PATIENT

by Bob Boardman

THE BOUGÉ

*Mutual trust is the surest basis of discipline in necessity and
danger.*

— Generals Fritsch & Beck, German Training Manual.

I didn't want to leave the Naval Hospital in Farragut, Idaho for
Philadelphia, about three thousand miles away. My home was
Salem, Oregon. It seemed unreasonable and unfair to be shipped to
the East Coast. The doctor at Farragut no doubt tried to explain
their limitations in what they could do for my neck wounds, but the

emotional trauma of going back east affected my reception of this idea. A specialist surgeon was needed.

Yes, they did have airplanes in those days. But I, accompanied by a corpsman, was put on a train for the long, tedious ride across the United States. Unknowingly, I had a one-year appointment with Dr. Clerf and his amazing laryngoscope and assortment of bougé, a medical ramrod-like instrument, designed to dilate the windpipe.

In my limited understanding of life as a twenty-one-year-old Marine, I could not comprehend how God wanted to stretch my perimeters, heart, vision and experience. Just as God did not ask my permission to slam a bullet through my neck and hand in that cane field in Okinawa, so He did not consult with me about a move to the City of Brotherly Love. He simply ordered it. Thankfully, His sovereignty knows and acts for the very best in our lives if we trust and wait for Him even without clear understanding.

The Philadelphia Naval Hospital, a gigantic medical complex, was overflowing with Navy and Marine casualties, especially from the recent horrendous battles of Iwo Jima and Okinawa. I shall never forget the trauma of seeing and meeting some of the endless multitudes of amputees, blind and maimed-for-life casualties.

On the forty-bed EENT (Eyes, Ears, Nose and Throat) open-bay ward, I soon met a tall, rangy rifleman from the First Marine Regiment, Robert Dean. This dark, wavy-haired, handsome Marine with his whispered Mississippi drawl had also been drilled through the neck on Okinawa by a Japanese sniper.

We conversed together by holding one finger over the tracheotomy tube in our necks that enabled us to breathe more freely. Plugging our trachs forced the air over our one functioning vocal chord and allowed us to communicate in soft, melodious Marine whispers. Our wounds had paralyzed one vocal chord and, when healed, the dense scar tissue in and around the windpipe required specialized, delicate surgery.

Back then, no Naval doctor knew this surgery technique, but they did effective scar revision surgery on us. However, in downtown Philly at Jefferson Memorial Hospital, a Dr. Clerf had helped perfect the laryngoscope along with bougé of various sizes.

About every two weeks Bob Dean and I were doped up on Nembutal, put in a Navy ambulance and driven to Jefferson Hospital. We were joined from the officer's ward by Marine Captain Tony LaRosa, whose neck was also severely mutilated by shrapnel. From all appearances, Tony's neck was in worse shape than ours. He ended up wearing his tracheotomy the rest of his life.

Bob, Tony and I had no idea what to expect from Dr. Clerf. He was a kind of gruff professional who didn't communicate a lot to us, but underneath we could sense he had our best interests at heart. He sprayed each of our throats with pontocane to deaden the surface. By turns, we lay down on a hard table with our head hanging over the end.

Dr. Clerf then put the laryngoscope down our throats, a hollow metal tube with a light on the end. I know how a sword swallower feels. When it was lined up with the trachea, he would say, "Relax. Now hold your breath!" Then he would plunge through the tube, a bougé slightly larger than our windpipes. This ramrod technique dilated the tracheas.

Then the kind and gentle doctor had a very special bougé as his ace in the hole. When this bougé went into the windpipe, small razorblade-like knives flicked out, breaking the skin of the trachea so that it would remain dilated and not constrict. The three of us went through this process about every two weeks for one year.

The key to all of this was not our own understanding, for that was very limited. It was to cooperate, trust and obey this skilled surgeon. "Hang your head over the end." "Relax!" "Hold your breath!" "Trust me."

So much of life is like this. My understanding is very limited—a move from Farragut to Philadelphia seemed so unreasonable; or the fearful bougé that three Marines couldn't clearly comprehend. In all of our lives we have inexplicable interruptions, delays, cancellations, losses, as well as unexpected opposition or broken relationships.

These are all the bougé of God as He attempts to dilate our shriveled, scarred hearts and enlarge them to contain His own vision, love, understanding and outlook.

If we walk by faith in God's promises in the Bible and His wisdom and ability to order all circumstances that would overpower us, He will cause them to ultimately work together for our good and for His glory. The adverse can be borne when we cooperate, trusting the skilled Master Surgeon, Jesus Christ, with His amazing assortment of bougé.

★   ★   ★

The Psychiatrist

Once the game is over the king and the pawn go back into the same box.

— Italian Proverb

During my eighteen months in various Naval hospitals following the battle of Okinawa in WWII, one year was spent in the US Naval Hospital in Philadelphia undergoing extensive, specialized surgery. I was a patient on the forty-bed EENT ward because of gunshot wounds to the neck and larynx while serving with C Company First Tank Battalion. Over that one year period, my voice and breathing gradually returned with each successive surgery.

One day a nurse told me I was "invited" to visit the commandant of the hospital. I was amazed and dumbfounded. I had only met one other Navy captain when one presented me with a combat award at the Naval Hospital in Farragut, Idaho. What could this commandant want with a lowly Marine corporal?

I donned my best hospital pajamas, slippers and bathrobe, and with much trepidation, made my way through the maze of corridors, wards and hallways in this gigantic medical complex to the Commandant's office.

The Navy captain received me kindly. He was the epitome of a man of that rank with his silver, well-groomed hair, cutting a trim figure in his white uniform. He listed slightly to the port side, so many medals decorated his blouse. He was a salty, career officer. Yes, he was the king and as a Marine enlisted man, I was a pawn.

"I've received a letter from your father in Salem, Oregon. He is deeply concerned about your becoming so religious during your time overseas. He requested us to have you examined by our chief psychiatrist. Would you consent to this exam?" The captain asked.

I could only whisper by placing my finger over the tracheotomy tube in my neck. I asked what the exam was like. The Captain, a doctor himself, replied, "You will be asked a few select questions and be evaluated on your answers. Then we'll send your father our evaluation."

"Sir, I am open and willing," I replied.

The next day I again traversed what seemed like miles of corridors, wondering what this encounter would be like. This was heavy stuff for someone in his early twenties and still in the process of recovering physically and emotionally.

This all started in the battle of Okinawa when I was evacuated to Guam aboard the USS *Solace,* then to San Francisco. From there I was transferred to Farragut, Idaho. Before being sent by train to Philadelphia, my father drove from Salem to Farragut to visit me.

I greatly anticipated our mini-family reunion, as I had left home at age eighteen, three years previously. Dad planned to stay three days, but cut his visit in half. He became very angry at my new-found faith and my awkward attempts to share it with him in whispers. Jesus promised that for people of personal faith in His deity, His sinless sacrifice at Calvary and His resurrection, some of their foes would be those of their own household.

My father had an outward form of religion, but rejected completely, until his deathbed conversion, the person of Christ as Savior, Creator and returning King of Kings and Judge of all the earth. He was saying, in essence, I do not want this man, Jesus, to reign over my son. Sadly, Dad had never known Christ by personal experience.

My Dad vented part of his anger through his letter requesting my psychiatric exam. I'm sure he wanted confirmation that I was a religious psycho. It hurt me that Dad's obsession with opposing my faith took priority over seeing or hoping for progress in my physical recovery. It increased the loneliness of being three thousand miles from home.

The chief psychiatrist in Philadelphia, a Navy commander, was kind but professional as he began his questions about my "religious experience." He carefully probed, "Do you see visions, do you hear audible voices? How did this religion come into your life?"

I whispered to him what I had experienced. "Sir, as a lost and helpless, sinful Marine on the road to destruction and God's judgment, I read a Gideon New Testament over a three-month period. I encountered Jesus Christ and realized for the first time His unconditional love for me by dying on the Cross. I received Him into my life on Goodenough Island in September 1943."

After I finished my story, the doctor amazed me by responding, "Son, I believe you are just fine and I'm going to write your father with this assurance." He was candid, "In fact, I personally wish that I could find this same kind of faith and heart peace. Will you pray for me?"

SCRIPTURE: *We had earthly fathers who disciplined us and we used to treat them with respect; how much more cheerfully should we submit to the Father of our spirits, and live! For they disciplined us only a short time...but He does it for our good, in order that we may share His holy character. — Hebrews 12.9,10*

PRAYER: *Lord Jesus Christ, I acknowledge You as the skilled Master Surgeon. As I trust You, help me to cooperate in this surgery, even though my understanding is very limited. Amen.*

THE SECRETARY OF THE NAVY
Washington, D.C. 20350-1000

The President of the United States takes pleasure in presenting the SILVER STAR MEDAL to

CORPORAL ROBERT R. BOARDMAN, JR.
UNITED STATES MARINE CORPS RESERVE

for service as set forth in the following

CITATION:

For conspicuous gallantry and intrepidity while serving as a Tank Driver of Company C, First Tank Battalion, First Marine Division, in action against enemy Japanese forces in Okinawa, Ryukyu Islands, 17 June 1945. While under heavy hostile machine-gun and mortar fire, Corporal Boardman left the protection of his tank and rode on the rear to give aid and support to a seriously wounded infantryman being taken to a forward aid station. Later, when his tank was hit and disabled by an enemy antitank gun and his Platoon Leader was seriously wounded, he voluntarily assisted in attempting to carry the stricken man to safety through extremely heavy hostile machine-gun and mortar fire. Although severely wounded, and left for dead during this endeavor, he made his way back to our lines. His outstanding courage and devotion to duty under fire were in keeping with the highest traditions of the United States Naval Service.

For the President,
/S/ JOHN L. SULLIVAN
Secretary of the Navy

⋆ **V** ⋆

Combat Equipment

The whole of military activity must relate directly or indirectly to the engagement. The end for which a soldier is recruited, clothed, armed and trained, the whole object of his sleeping, eating, drinking and marching is simply that he should fight at the right place and the right time.

— Major General Carl von Clausewitz
On War, 1832

Sketch by Arnie Lyshall

Twenty

782 GEAR

by Bob Boardman

Don't borrow someone else's armor. Use what you have been given, even though simple and humble. Prove your own weapon and equipment.

—R. Boardman

Ask any Marine—Reserve, Regular, past or present—what "782 Gear" means and he will know. In essence, he will say: *782 Gear consists of equipment that is essential to combat life.*

Furthermore, he can still give you a pretty accurate list of these items that help Marines to be ready to accomplish their mission:

Flak jacket, helmet, first-aid kit, canteen (2), canteen cover (2), canteen cup, knit cap, E-tool (entrenching), poncho with liner, modular sleeping bag, shelter half with pins and poles, magazine pouches with magazines, M16A2 service rifle, etc.

Several items differ from WWII and the Korean War era Marines. We didn't have flak jackets or glove shells and inserts. Canvas leggings and bayonets were part of our 782 Gear.

During Marine boot camp and afterwards in our respective line company training, we were so thoroughly indoctrinated and so frequently inspected on our 782 Gear that we can't forget these items even today. That essential equipment is part and parcel of why we became Marines!

Marines may not care to admit it, but like everyone else, we do collect nonessentials. Take a look in a Marine's footlocker or closet. How do we measure nonessentials? By knowing what is the task of the Marine Corps. It is to be ready at a moment's notice to defend our nation against any threat to our national security, freedom and liberty.

When a Marine moves out to fulfil his basic task, he does so with his 782 Gear. That does not include personal camera, civilian clothes, pictures of loved ones, diary, video camera, stereo player with tapes and CDs, souvenirs, personal vehicle, etc.

Believe it or not, it does not include those colorful dress blues and shoes with mirror-like shine. It does not include decorative medals and ribbons, even if he holds the Medal of Honor. War-fighting requires only the equipment essential to combat life.

A military base can also easily gather nonessentials. A few months ago on a base I noted the following buildings and departments that to me seemed strange and out of place in relation to going to war or national defense:

Hdqtrs. Element, Base Club System; Instructional Management School; Intervention and Treatment Branch; Free Tax Preparation Bldg. Then there was the huge shopping mall that included the ubiquitous fast-food shops: Subway, Dominos, Wendy's, the Golden Arches and Burger King.

On that base I met a Marine as he stepped out of his pretty red pickup. It had a bumper sticker that read: *Marines, the World's 911 Force*. I asked him if he thought the above buildings and departments contributed toward being a 911 force. He sheepishly shook his head in the negative.

I ate on a non-Marine base not too long ago in one of the best chow halls I've ever experienced. In fact, they are competing for the best food and service among all bases nationwide. This is excellent for morale, competition and calories, but has little to do with essentials in defending our country and defeating the enemy.

In the final analysis, winning limited or extensive wars comes down to a few good men with hearts afire to serve their country and one another, with a will to win—and equipped with essentials for combat, their 782 Gear.

In the realm of the spiritual, the principles are the same. There are essential accoutrements for waging and winning spiritual warfare. This is our spiritual 782 Gear, less tangible than that of the Marine Corps, but nonetheless vital:

The Bible, which is called the Sword of the Holy Spirit. It is spiritual seed that brings about a new birth when planted, watered and nourished in a receptive heart. It is also essential daily spiritual food for the warrior of God. He stands upon the command that man does not live by bread alone but by every Word of God.

Prayer is our communication lifeline to our great Commander-in-Chief and His Executive Officer, Jesus Christ. Our petitions, thanksgiving, praise and our deepest heart concerns and worries can be offered before His presence day or night.

An Eternity-based awareness and lifestyle that sees the things of this world as temporal and soon to fade away. The Christian soldier recognizes the spiritual realm as the truly real world that lasts forever.

A clear Bible-based warrior's armor, or spiritual 782 Gear, is laid out in the New Testament letter of Ephesians 6.10-18. It includes a description of our deadly enemy and all the resources we need for victory. Let us not be encumbered with "religious" nonessentials.

☆ ☆ ☆

SCRIPTURE: *Put on God's full armor [782 Gear], so as to be able to take a stand in the day when evil attacks you... — Ephesians 6.13*

PRAYER: *Help me, Lord God, not to be encumbered with religious nonessentials, but rather to be equipped with the entire 782 Gear as a soldier of Christ. Amen.*

Sketch by Arnie Lyshall

Twenty-One

THE PASSWORD

by Bob Boardman

Communications dominate war; broadly considered, they are the most important single element in strategy, political or military.

— Rear Adm. Alfred Mahan, 1900

During combat in WWII in the Pacific, the enemy was often a skilled infiltrator and night fighter. Because of this, Marine units found it necessary to adopt a different password for identification every night. In the First Marine Division, before nightfall, the password was sent out verbally through the regiments, battalions, companies and on down to platoons, squads, weapons-served units and tank crews. Every man knew that usually simple, but vital, one word. Sometimes a double word was used like Harley-Davidson.

Each night your very life depended on knowing that word.

Make one move after dark without that all-important password, no matter how good your purpose or urgent your mission, and you are a dead man.

Challenger: *"Halt, who goes there?"* followed by the ominous click of the safety being released on a M-1 rifle, carbine, Tommy gun or .45 pistol.

"It's me, your buddy, Joe," comes back a nervously whispered answer.

"Gimme the password," demands the sentry.

For those who had either forgotten or never received the magic word, it meant life or death. You earnestly prayed that the challenger was a reasonable guy and not a green, trigger-happy Marine.

Sprinkled here and there among casualty lists from WWII are men who forgot the password or some who tried in vain to talk or joke their way back to their foxhole without it. There are a few who incredulously refused to give it, arrogantly claiming that the challenger certainly knew who they were. What an ignominious way to die or receive a Purple Heart!

There were certain English words containing the letter *L* that most Japanese had difficulty pronouncing: They tended to make an *R* sound out of an *L*. Someone in Division Headquarters who understood this Japanese peculiarity and had an ample vocabulary came up with words that meant life to Marines and death to the enemy.

For some reason, I vividly remember some of those passwords, especially from the battle of Peleliu in September and October 1944. Victory hung in the balance for days on that blood-drenched coral atoll. Here are some of those passwords with the way most Japanese would pronounce them in parentheses.

Chevrolet *(Sheburorei)*; lollipop *(roripoppu)*; Cadillac *(Kajirakku)*; Harley-Davidson *(Hare-Dabidoson)*; baseball *(besubaru)*; holiday *(horidei)*; rebellion *(riberion)*; Lilliputian *(riripuchian)*.

With the word *Lilliputian*, I can imagine this scene between a couple of Marines just behind the front lines:

"Look Kilroy, how the (blank) should I know what Lilliputian means. We're not paid to know. Just try saying it once more!"

"Sarge, if I can't pronounce it, how can the (blankety-blank) Japs say it? Can't I just use last night's password?"

"No, Kilroy, not if you want to live to see another day! Now let's try Lilliputian again. Wait a minute, there's someone who will know— Say, Lieutenant, you went to Yale didn't you…?"

Use of a hard-to-pronounce password to confound and discover the enemy is many centuries old. In the book of Judges in the Old Testament, two warring factions spoke the same language, but their pronunciation differed on certain words.

Remnants of the defeated Ephraimites tried to escape through the fords of the Jordan River being guarded by the Gileadites. When they approached this narrow, closely guarded escape route, they were asked one by one:

"Are you an Ephraimite?" If he answered *"No,"* he was then commanded, *"Say 'Shibboleth.'"* If he pronounced the word *"Sibboleth,"* they knew he was lying and an enemy. Inability to say the password correctly cost the man his life. Thousands of Ephraimites were killed at that time.

Is it necessary to know a password in order to enter into the presence of God as a permanent citizen of His Kingdom?

God in His infinite love and mercy upon us wandering, earthbound rebels has given to us His open-secret password.

Jesus Christ is the password.

Knowing Him enables us to pass the sentry's challenge to enter into God's presence. He Himself said, *"I am the Way, the Truth and the Life. No one comes to the Father except through Me."* — John 14.6

True repentance and heart-belief in Jesus Christ's life, sacrificial death, glorious resurrection and ascension guarantee the forgiveness of our wrongdoing and eternal safety with God forever.

SCRIPTURE: *Keep on praying in the Spirit with every kind of prayer and entreaty, at every opportunity, be ever on the alert with perfect devotion and entreaty for all God's people. — Ephesians 6.18*

PRAYER: *Lord, give me spiritual discernment to be able to test the spirits and to know clearly who is the enemy and who is a true follower of Jesus Christ. Amen.*

D. Enright

Twenty-Two

THE GYROSTABILIZER

by Bob Boardman

The men who followed Him were unique in their generation. They turned the world upside down because their hearts had been turned right side up. The world has never been the same.

— Billy Graham

After an accelerated wartime seven-week Marine boot camp in early 1943, hundreds of us in our new green uniforms and our equipment packed in khaki-colored seabags were sent by ten-wheel trucks to Camp Elliott on the outskirts of San Diego for infantry training. Camp Pendleton had not opened yet.

In other chapters I've told how after initial infantry training, we were "volunteered" alphabetically for tank school. I sometimes wonder what would have happened to me if my last name was Zaring!

As new prospective tankers we were sent off to Jaques Farm, an old fruit orchard, for training. Never mind that some of us were well over six feet and could hardly squeeze into the fifteen-ton light tanks of that day.

We trained in light tanks and when we were shipped to Australia in mid-1943 we joined C Company First Tank Battalion in Ballarat, Australia. Those were also light tanks. In fact, they had to be started by placing a large cartridge in a cylinder and firing it to turn over the engine.

The First Marine Division invaded Cape Gloucester, New Britain on 26 December 1943. Our C Company still had light tanks. A .50 caliber bullet could pierce the side armor. A and B Companies, however, had replaced their light tanks with M4A2, 33-ton (fully loaded) medium Shermans.

After the Gloucester battle, my company's tanks were replaced with medium Shermans, so that for the battle of Peleliu, the entire First Tank Battalion was equipped with M4A2 with twin diesel engines. These steel monsters were awesome weapons on both Peleliu and Okinawa. Benis Frank describes the vital part tanks had in the battle of Okinawa:

> *Ground assault operations…were the special province of the armored and infantry units. Concerning the armored support of his 6th Division Marines, General Shepherd wrote,* "If any one supporting arm can be singled out as having contributed more than any others during the progress of the campaign, the tank would certainly be selected." *In a battle lesson issued to his 32nd Army, Lt. General Ushijima supported this theme, stating that* "The enemy's power lies in his tanks. It has become obvious that our general battle against the American forces is a battle against their tanks."

One of the keys to the effectiveness of both the Army and Marine Corps Sherman tanks was a little six by eight inch black box called the gyrostabilizer that was mounted alongside the 75mm cannon and coaxial .30 caliber machine gun in the 15-ton turret.

The gyrostabilizer was one of WWII's best-kept secrets. Our five-man crew had clear, urgent instructions that if we ever had to abandon tank, the gyrostabilizer was the first and most important item to be destroyed. Also, the firing pin in the 75mm cannon was to be removed and the back plates on all the machine guns were to be dismantled.

There was a vital purpose to that little black box. As the tank was underway, often over extremely steep and rough terrain, the gyroscope inside the box, spinning in a vertical plane, kept the turret guns steady and level. No matter how much the tank bounced around, up and down, the gunner could stay on his target and fire on the move.

The gyrostabilizer gave us an unprecedented advantage in moving combat. Before its marvelous inception, tanks usually had to fully stop in order for the gunner to come on target. This made the tank a target itself.

In my own life I need a gyrostabilizer for the ups and downs of daily living. It seems there is much rough terrain, both small rocky bumps and great gullies. Right in my own home and family or with close loved ones and friends, I need steadiness.

Or in the course of my work there are plenty of rough spots and unexpected challenges. The loss of position, an incompatible boss or coworker puts my attitude to the test. The loss of my job. Or how about sickness, a serious illness or loss of a loved one? All of the above can be very rough terrain. What, or better yet, *who* gives you and me true stability?

Jesus Christ is God's amazing Gyrostabilizer. He can and will keep us level and stable when we trust Him and cast upon Him all of our cares, anxieties and needs daily, for it deeply matters to Him about you and about me.

SCRIPTURE: *I will try to walk a blameless path, but how I need Your help, especially in my own home, where I long to act as I should.* — *Psalm 101:2*

PRAYER: *You, Lord, are the God of all circumstances, the ups and downs of daily living. Make Jesus Christ to be my Gyrostabilizer to keep me level and stable for Your glory. Amen.*

⋆ **VI** ⋆

Forgiveness, Repentance and Restoration

Edith Cavell's last words:

This I would say, standing in view of God and Eternity: I realize that patriotism is not enough; I must have no hatred and bitterness toward anyone.

— Edith Cavell, 12 October 1915, to the chaplain attending her execution by German firing squad

Pfc. Charles Holsinger,
US Army, the
Philippines, 1945

Chuck Holsinger at home
in Upland, Indiana

Twenty-Three

THE LONG MARCH TO FORGIVENESS

Charles D. Holsinger's Story

There is a tragedy in the lives of many soldiers and civilians who have endured trauma. Basically it is the unwillingness to bring personal issues out into the open, confess them, and move on with their lives. This is true of Americans as well as Filipinos. This lack of forgiveness has ruined individuals and families. I have a dear friend who told me that her father was a US fighter pilot in the Pacific during World War II. He would never talk about his experiences. His only expressions were outbursts against the Japanese who had taken four years out of his life! He was so angry at them that he took it out on his family. He ended up making life miserable for everyone.

— C.D. Holsinger

Introduction by R. Boardman: In my mind Chuck Holsinger is one of the great ones from WWII. He endured 165 days (five and a half months) of consecutive combat against the Japanese in the Philippines, serving as an infantryman in the Twenty-Fifth Division. He was decorated with the Silver Star, our nation's third highest award, for gallantry in action (see citation at end of chapter).

But there is something that makes this time unique, above and beyond Chuck's combat experience, amazing as that is. This is his journey to complete forgiveness of his former enemy, the Japanese soldiers and people. This was, indeed, a long march that took years, as it did many of us who engaged the Japanese Imperial Forces in no-quarter combat.

I first met Chuck on Okinawa after the war in 1955. Jean and I lived there as missionaries for four years before moving up to the Japan mainland to live and work for the next thirty years. Chuck was visiting Okinawa for a few days on a speaking mission.

Because he was a fellow combat warrior, I did something I didn't do with many people. I took him from Naha, where we lived, down south to Kunishi Ridge and showed him the spot where a number of us from C Company were wounded and almost lost our lives behind the Japanese lines on 17 June 1945. Here we were conversing on the spot ten years later.

Chuck's first question to me was, "Bob, how can you come back and share the Gospel with these people, after being maimed for life by them?" According to Chuck my answer startled him. "A wound like this is no worse than my sins. God forgave me my sins, so why should I not forgive the Japanese? Chuck, these scars are beauty marks. They are like the nailprints in Jesus' hands. Those wounds are my credentials to the Japanese people that I have forgiven them."

I personally had no idea of the great ongoing struggle to forgive the Japanese that was going on deep in the inner recesses of Chuck's heart or what my answer did to him. He said, "It was a powerful statement that left me in silence." Our simple words and actions can be used by the Living God to minister and help those with great heart needs. Chuck still had miles and some years to go on his long march to forgiveness, but I'm grateful that this experience at Kunishi Ridge was one stepping stone toward victory.

After a light campaign in the Northern Solomon Islands, the Twenty-Fifth Army Division transitioned through New Caledonia to prepare for their landing on Luzon, the Philippines, on 11 January 1945. Here are several parts of Chuck Holsinger's extraordinary story of those 165 days of consecutive combat.

Moving into hill country and up Highway 5, the fighting became very intense. We were losing so many men it began to look like we would all be gone in a matter of a few days. The normal size of a platoon at full strength was forty men. We were down to eight! Our company was at half strength—about one hundred men.

The wounded and the dead had been accounted for—the dead were bagged, and the wounded were readied for evacuation. And now it was time to move men up in rank. I thought it was my time for advancement. But the first sergeant had other plans because he had friends. Two other men, Williams and Frank, were promoted to staff sergeant/squad leader and buck sergeant/assistant squad leader instead of me.

In late afternoon we dug our foxholes at specific places assigned by the first sergeant. Frank and Williams were placed at the ends of the squad to dig in, since they were now in positions of leadership. The remaining seven men in the squad were given assignments between these two men. That night I bedded down in my hole with anger and disgust at the first sergeant—and I was blaming God, too.

After all, I had seniority!

In the middle of the night the silence was shattered by the explosion of enemy mortar fire. The attack was sudden and over very quickly. All of us were immediately covered with dust and the smell of exploding shells. This is when soldiers feel frustrated—the enemy had attacked, but we had no one to shoot at! After the initial shells had crashed and exploded, there was silence for a moment, and then cries of anguish and pain from those who were wounded.

In the morning I learned that Frank, the man who had been promoted to buck sergeant and assistant squad leader before me, had his arm blown off. For all intents and purposes, I should have been in his foxhole. But now I was to be moved up. My rank now was buck sergeant, and my position was second in command, which meant I would bring up the rear of the squad rather than being the one out in front. My days as a scout were over.

The assignment for the day was to attack a series of bunkers that anchored a Japanese defense line. Williams, now staff sergeant, although with less seniority, was to lead the attack. It should have been my turn to lead. But no, once again it would be my time to wait.

The two scouts were sent out ahead, with Sergeant Williams immediately following them. Within minutes there was heavy rifle and cannon fire and a raging battle. Sergeant Williams was blown into eternity.

Above the din of the battle, the captain shouted, "Holsinger, move up and take charge!" In less than twelve hours I had moved from private first class to staff sergeant. God knew where He wanted me to be and when.

On 28 February 1945, on a hill near Maringalo, Nueva Ecija—about three kilometers west of Diddig—our company of soldiers

(down to about 150 men) was to occupy a small hill that was shaped like a pear. It was late in the afternoon when our six-man squad dug in "V" formation—three men on one side and three on the other side of the small end of the "pear." My hole was near the point of the "V."

Little did we know that a large detachment of the enemy was about 130 meters away. Under a bush on a little knoll was an observation point from which a person in a prone position could watch our every move. (We learned this a day later, when we captured the knoll.)

It was about 1:30 A.M. The night had been clear, but now a thick layer of clouds covered the sky. The light of the moon had disappeared. I was awake on guard duty on my side of the "V." In low tones the man who was on duty on the other side and I talked briefly. Everything seemed to be OK. I didn't know that in a matter of minutes that man would be dead.

To keep myself alert, I worked on memorizing Bible verses and whole chapters during the night watches. On this very night I was working on Psalm 91, and reviewing Matthew chapters 5, 6 and 7—

the Sermon on the Mount. With the light of the moon gone, I stood up, stretched, and then sat down on the edge of my hole. Peace and quietness ruled the evening.

Suddenly I heard a scuffle, then frightening screams and shouts that pierced the night air from the three members of our squad who were on the other side, about five yards away. There was the clashing of steel as bayonets, rifles and helmets smashed together. There wasn't time for the men to point their rifles and fire. They were fighting with their fists and anything that they could get their hands on. Sickening cries of anguish and agony filled the darkness. I could hear the strange and eerie sounds of the dying coming from Americans and Japanese alike.

It was a well-planned attack. The enemy had used the night darkness to try to destroy us. They had chosen to attack at what they thought was the most vulnerable, and yet most strategic point. Soon they were occupying the foxholes of my comrades. There were thuds, as bodies of my comrades were thrown out of their holes. I looked and saw only darkness.

Then against the skyline I caught a glimpse of a raised bayonet ready to strike. I concentrated my rifle fire on the lone figure. It disappeared. I swung my rifle around and began spraying the five-yard space between my side and near my three comrades.

Instinct told me that my comrades were dead, and that it was important to hold our position at any cost. I cried out to the Lord for help—to clear my mind and settle my nerves.

Now the enemy focused its attack on the three of us on my side. In minutes my sergeant was wounded, and crawled back to the safety of the main body of our troops, on the higher ground behind us.

The enemy now began to throw grenades at the two of us who were left. I could hear the fuses sizzle as the grenades rolled by, only inches away. It would be only a matter of time before they would hit our holes.

As we heard the next pop of the start of a grenade, we started counting. We had three seconds. Then it happened—a grenade fell into my comrade's hole and exploded on his back. I called to him but there was no answer. The blinding dust from the exploding grenade engulfed us.

There wasn't time to even try and see if my partner, Jake, was alive, so I continued firing at the enemy. A short time later I heard a groan and I shouted for a medic. One brave man crawled out on his stomach and pulled Jake to the safety of the perimeter and higher ground.

The situation was now too dangerous for any movement of personnel. The whole American line was awake and tense in the darkness. I could hear the Japanese talking—when there were no shouts from our own men and when there was a break in the din of exploding shells, the chatter of machine guns and rifle fire.

My thoughts were racing—*did the Japanese know that I was alone? Would they rush at me?* If they did, it would be all over. In the terror of the moment I cried out to the Lord for help—especially to calm my pounding heart. There was instant peace, knowing that whether I lived or died I belonged to the Lord.

The Lord gave me a thought—I had one last option. I shouted for support: "Give me mortar fire!" My only hope was for the mortar men to pull the shells in so close that they would explode in the five-yard area that was between me and the enemy on the other side. I was counting on the exploding mortar shells to keep the enemy at bay.

The mortar shells were coming in dangerously close. Every explosion created clouds of thick dust and smoke that made it difficult to breathe. I waited until I could hear the whistle of the falling shells, then I ducked into the shelter of my hole as the explosion covered me with dirt. After every explosion, I came up firing my rifle.

I prayed that God would enable me to hang on until daybreak. I knew that daylight would be my salvation. About an hour later, another soldier joined me with a bag of grenades. Three hours later streaks of light filled the sky. Morning was here. I was still alive but my ammunition was almost gone.

The Japanese were now talking excitedly and there was movement. They were grunting and struggling as they tried to retreat with their dead and wounded. They disappeared in the early morning shadows.

Daylight exposed the carnage. Two of my buddies were dead, their bodies scattered among the corpses of the enemy. A third comrade, whose hole was with the men who died, had his right hand almost severed when he grabbed a Japanese bayonet by the blade and kept it from being thrust into his heart.

After crouching for over three hours, I could hardly stand on my cramped legs. I looked in my own foxhole and saw two mortar fins. They reminded me of how close death had come.

The captain congratulated me, "You single-handedly saved the company by holding your ground. I am putting you in for a medal."

For me the whole event was a miracle! God had spared my life.

About a month later I received letters from my father in Oakland, California and my brother in Wheaton, Illinois. By Asian time reckoning, both had an urge to pray for me. My father asked his boss to excuse him so that he could pray for his son. And my brother left his college classroom to pray. The timing was exactly right. The two were simultaneously praying for me as I was under fire.

The captain was mistaken. I was not alone and I did not do it single-handedly. God was with me. Later on when the Philippines was secured and we were pulled off the lines, I was decorated with the Silver Star medal by our commanding general. The citation read in part "…for gallantry in action against the enemy…bravery…courage."

The men congratulated me as a hero, but I didn't feel that way. I had done what every soldier was expected to do.

Perhaps the most important message to get across is that one cannot have a healthy life without forgiveness. Pain and suffering must be talked about and faced. The ugliness of war and any other bad incident can leave either ugly scars or beauty marks. The choice is up to us. I chose to turn my scars into beauty marks.

But there is another reason for writing. While still a young man, I made the decision to make God a part of my life—whether I lived or died. For some reason or another God spared my life. Some of my closest friends—even Christian buddies—died in the battlefields of the Southwest Pacific. On more than one occasion I have had to ask, "Lord, why them and not me?"

The Lord has a path for each one of us to walk. My path has been very clear, serving the Lord as a missionary since 1953. I am alive today because of His mercy and goodness. I do not see myself favored because I came through the war without a scratch. Rather I recognize a responsibility to make sure that I be and do (to the best of my ability) what I know God called me to be and to do. One of the things I should do is to write this account.

I learned early on that it is important to talk about the war. I had kept everything to myself, thinking that no one would understand. However, getting these things out into the open brings a sense of "cleansing" in my heart and a positive response from others.

— From Chuck Holsinger's book *Above the Cry of Battle*,
ACW Press 2001, ISBN 1-892525-55-0

✫   ✫   ✫

SCRIPTURE: *You must remove all bitterness, rage, anger, loud threats and insults, with all malice. You must practice being kind to one another, tenderhearted, forgiving one another, just as God through Christ has graciously forgiven you. – Ephesians 4.31,32*

PRAYER: *Gracious Lord, give me courage in battle when my life and the lives of my comrades are on the line. But also, and just as difficult, give me moral courage to forgive others as Christ has forgiven me. For His name's sake. Amen.*

✫   ✫   ✫

25th INFANTRY DIVISION
Office of the Commanding General

25 June 1945

AWARD OF THE SILVER STAR

By direction of the President, under the provision of the act of Congress approved 9 July 1918, (Bul 43,WD, 1918), a Silver Star is awarded by the Commanding General, 25th Infantry Division, to the following named enlisted man:

Private First Class Charles D. Holsinger,
16170833, Infantry, United States Army

For gallantry in action against the Japanese forces at Maringalu, Luzon, Philippine Islands on 28 February 1945. During a night attack upon his company position, the enemy infiltrated into the six-man strong point of which Private First Class HOLSINGER was a member. After killing two men, wounding one and forcing one to withdraw, the enemy occupied the four positions to his left and concentrated rifle fire and grenades upon him. Although he was now alone, with no thought of retreat he coolly returned fire and directed assault mortar fire on the enemy not more than five yards from his position. He held his position for one hour until joined by another soldier carrying hand grenades. At dawn he assisted in clearing the enemy from the positions they had taken.

Private First Class HOLSINGER'S gallant actions in the face of grave danger, which limited the enemy's infiltration and enabled his platoon to hold its ground, were in keeping with the highest traditions of the military service.

BY COMMAND OF MAJOR GENERAL MULLINS,
United States Army

Lt. Dave Legg, US Army,
Vietnam, 1967

Dave and wife Terri
with grandchild in
Colorado Springs
today. Navigator
staff.

Twenty-Four

THE BRAVEST MAN I NEVER KNEW

Dave Legg's Story

One man with Courage makes a majority.
— Attributed to Andrew Jackson, 1767-1845

I took ROTC (Reserve Officer's Training Corps) in college because I needed the $30 a month that paid for groceries. Also, I had always thought I might enjoy military life, as I had been an Eagle Scout. I did well and graduated with a Regular Army Commission.

I found that Army life did agree with me and I soon developed my life goal of becoming an Army general. I had all of the right assignments—company commander in the 101st Airborne, instructor at the infantry school, and all the necessary career courses.

My first tour in Vietnam was with MACV (Military Assistance Command VN) as a regional advisor on a six-man team. We lived with the Vietnamese troops and spoke Vietnamese. It was on this assignment that I encountered the bravest man I never knew.

For most people, fear of the unknown is one of their greatest nemeses. That was true of me as I left my wife and five-year-old son for Vietnam in the summer of 1967.

Courage is difficult to describe, but unmistakable when you see it. It has been defined as that quality which enables a person to proceed in the face of danger with calmness and firmness. Someone once said that courage is only learned in the context of risk and the possibility of failure. General George Patton believed that courage is directly proportionate to how we respond to our fears. It was that belief that led him to develop his lifelong principle, "never take counsel of your fears."

If that is the meaning of courage, I once knew a very courageous man. That's not exactly true because I never actually met this man, but I did personally observe his actions in a life-threatening situation.

This story began in 1967 in Kontum province, Vietnam. I was assigned to the Military Assistance Command as an advisor to the Vietnamese District Chief. Major Bang was in command of five infantry companies and a 155mm artillery battery. Together we lived in a defensive compound about five miles outside of Kontum city in the central highlands. As we prepared to bed down the evening of 31 January, our intelligence reports indicated no major enemy units in our vicinity. What has come to be known as the Tet Offensive began that evening. Early the next morning our compound came under an intense mortar attack. As dawn broke we were greeted with the news that the 124th NVA Regiment had occupied Kontum city and had placed an infantry battalion in a small nearby village to block the road that led from our compound into the city. Obviously they wanted us to stay out of the city!

We decided to assume the offensive by sending two infantry companies into the village in a reconnaissance-by-force to assess the situation and determine how we could take our companies into the city to reinforce the besieged MACV compound. Major Bang requested that I accompany the infantry units to assist with close air support if needed. It was.

As we entered the village we came under intense small arms and machine-gun fire and began to take casualties. We soon found ourselves pinned down in a banana grove by an entrenched enemy and unable to maneuver. I called for close air support that was normally plentiful and readily available. This time it wasn't. With most major cities and units in South Vietnam under attack, nothing was available. Normally, F-4 fighter jets dropping napalm, canister bombs and firing 20mm cannons would be quick to respond. On this day our only response was from an Air Force forward air controller flying a single engine L-19 and armed only with marking rockets! These were meant only to mark, not destroy targets.

The customary role of forward air controllers was to communicate with the troops on the ground and direct the fighters to the target. As a group of pilots, they were extremely brave and took a lot of risks but they didn't typically personally engage the enemy units. We were soon to learn that there wasn't anything typical about this pilot.

Soon after arriving on the scene, the FAC could see that our situation was desperate. Banana trees provide very little protection against AK47 rifles and machine guns. We heard the sound of a plane in a dive followed by two small explosions. We watched in amazement as this small single engine propeller plane continued to dive on the enemy position firing marking rockets. When he had fired all of his marking rockets, he continued to dive on the enemy position firing his M16 rifle out the window. When he ran out of ammunition he continued this assault dropping hand grenades!

These relentless assaults from the air caused two things. The enemy stopped firing at us and began firing at the plane and we were able to maneuver out of the banana grove and flank the enemy position. Then the plane disappeared as quickly as it had arrived.

It is difficult for me to comprehend the bravery I saw demonstrated that day. That's the kind of thing we read about or see in the movies, but I witnessed it first-hand. I saw a very brave man demonstrate incredible courage without "taking counsel of his fears."

Several nights later, sitting alone in a bunker during a mortar attack, I found myself wondering what happens to us after we die. I found myself recalling stories from Sunday school and wondering if they were true. I didn't find "foxhole religion" that night, but as is the case for many combat soldiers, my experiences in Vietnam caused me to have some pretty significant questions about life and death. I came home after my first tour to attend the Infantry Officer's Career Course at Fort Benning, Georgia. This course prepared junior officers for ascending the ladder of leadership as a career. I brought with me a nagging question—"What happens to us after we die?" Fear of the unknown had come home with me. I can remember sitting in class at the Infantry School and daydreaming about my future. I saw myself retired and having accomplished my career goals. I had paid a high price to become a retired Army general. At that point I can remember having a persistent question. Is that all there is? There had to be more to life than just working hard, sacrificing to accomplish career goals, retiring and dying.

One day at a picnic a fellow officer asked me a startling question. He asked if I was a Christian. I replied, "I think so." At that time I thought anyone who was an American and believed in God and the Bible was a Christian. He explained that the Bible teaches that Christians have a personal relationship with Jesus Christ. One thing I was sure of was that I didn't have a personal relationship with Jesus. I committed my life to Christ that day and my life hasn't been the same since.

When I returned to Vietnam for a second tour as a company commander with the 101st Airborne Division, I saw more death and dying, bravery and courage, but this time there was a significant difference. I had the answer to my question. I knew there was life after death. I no longer had to fear the unknown.

☆　☆　☆

SCRIPTURE: *This is the testimony; God has given us eternal life, and this life is in His Son. He who has the Son has life; he who does not have the Son of God does not have life. — 1 John 5.11,12*

PRAYER: *Heavenly Father, thank You for providing for me as a free gift Your Son, Jesus Christ. I am joyfully in debt to you forever. Amen.*

☆　☆　☆

HEADQUARTERS
UNITED STATES MILITARY ASSISTANCE COMMAND,
VIETNAM
APO San Francisco 96222

GENERAL ORDERS   6 June 1968
NUMBER 1593

AWARD OF THE BRONZE STAR MEDAL
(FIRST OAK LEAF CLUSTER)

1. TC 320. The following AWARD is announced.

LEGG, JOHN D. OF105220 (SSAN 409-68-9221) CPT INF USA
Awarded: Bronze Star Medal (First Oak Leaf Cluster) with "V" Device
Date action: 30 January 2 – February 1968
Theater: Republic of Vietnam
Reason: For heroism in connection with military operations against a hostile force: Captain Legg distinguished himself by heroic action from 30 January to 2 February 1968 while serving as an Advisor to the Kontum District Headquarters and the 140th Regional Force Company, Republic of Vietnam. During that period, a North Vietnamese Army battalion attacked the District Headquarters with mortar and small arms fire and occupied the nearby hamlet of Phuong Quy. Captain Legg, with no thought for his own safety, directed counter-fire, preventing the enemy from gaining entrance to the headquarters. During subsequent patrols into hostile areas, he actively engaged the enemy and assisted the patrol leader in destroying positions, capturing enemy equipment, and obtaining valuable documents. Captain Legg's conduct during this period was characterized by extreme aggressiveness and outstanding leadership and lent confidence to the Vietnamese soldiers. Captain Legg's heroic actions were in keeping with the highest traditions of the United States Army and reflect great credit upon himself and the military service.
Authority: By direction of the President under the provisions of Executive Order 11046, 24 August 1962.

Rob Wood today lives
in Everett, Washington

Twenty-Five

NIGHT AMBUSH–
CONFESSIONS OF
A VIETNAM VET

by Rob Wood with Bob Boardman

A letter from a Vietnam veteran to a WWII Marine. As surely as spring follows a bitter winter, hope can emerge from the pain, tragedy and suffering of war and its aftermath.

Dear Bob,

It is hard to write my story. I've started many times. But I get going and feel this huge weight crushing down on me. It is very difficult for me to describe this powerful force that bound me for twenty-eight years, but here goes.

I had never told anyone about Vietnam—I mean the real Vietnam. The fear, coupled with the boredom was incredible. I was an electronics technician ten miles north of Danang. My tour was about over and the only war I had experienced was on the receiving end of mortar and rocket attacks.

I wanted to be what I enlisted to be, a combat Marine. I trained my replacement and volunteered for patrol duty. I started out checking Vietnamese ID cards in several surrounding villages. Then it was night patrols. This was different.

We were told of NVA (enemy) activity in the area. One night we spotted movement, so set up a hasty ambush and waited. I took out the first man. There were tracers going everywhere. Someone screamed to stop shooting. We had ambushed one of our own patrols! Their point man was a friend of mine and I was told that he was hurt very badly. For seventeen years I stuffed this incident deep within and then I lost control and my life shattered like a piece of glass. I needed to talk about it. It was all wrong and was something that wasn't supposed to happen.

When I returned from Vietnam I discovered my fiancé was eight months pregnant by another man. I didn't know this until she greeted me when I got off the plane. But I was a Marine and I could handle anything—and I did for awhile. She had the baby adopted by another family and we finally married. Over eighteen years, the past continually worked on destroying our relationship. Finally, when two hundred Marines were uselessly killed in an undefended position in Beirut, I woke up to the trauma I had suppressed for so many years.

I then was divorced. This was wrong, too. We had three children. The scars were opening up that I had hidden. No one understood. I wanted help because I was trained to survive. The pain was incredible. I don't know whether it was the divorce or just my whole life caving in on me.

I only survived because of the faint thought that it would be horrible for my kids to have a father that took his own life. Today I know that God had his hand on me even during that time. No matter how deep the depression, something helped me climb out of the deep, slippery abyss.

Bob, all of this is so painful. Then the Lord blessed me with a wonderful second wife. But I had no basis to build a marriage on. It, too, began falling apart. Satan was in control.

Then I met Jesus Christ.

It was only when I stood with tears running down my face, listening to the son of a friend talk about the forgiveness of God that was freely available to me through Jesus Christ that I came to myself.

Knowing Jesus Christ gave me a new strength. I had become a heavy drinker to anesthetize my pain. As soon as I got rid of the pain and guilt, I was able to walk away from alcohol. I always thought a Marine could shoulder anything until I found out that men of strength don't carry excess baggage. People of true strength have help from God.

The pain of my second failed marriage does not fill me with anger. It just fills me with sadness. I struggle with human loneliness. It is hard to write this because it's hard to be alone. Satan almost destroyed me with the weight of guilt. But through my Heavenly Father's Word, Christ is turning it into a foundational stone in my life. I didn't understand how adversity could be a gift until I met Jesus Christ.

Please pray that the Lord would bless me with a helpmate, a friend, a lover—the wife that I need, if it is His will. When my second marriage ended it was pure agony, but God has used this pain to truly bless me. This suffering has guided me into understanding the true meaning of life through Christ, a question I have pondered since I was a child.

I don't like to write these difficult things because sometimes the story of survival for me during those dark times is something many people find difficult to handle. The Marine Corps trained me well, thank God, and that helped in the survival process.

Please pray for my three children and for my divorced spouses. Pray that they also come to truly know the Lord. Thanks so much.

Sincerely your friend,
Rob

P.S. I pray that your family's lives stay blessed. If I copy this over I won't mail it.

✯✯✯

SCRIPTURE: *Therefore if any man be in Christ, he is a new creation; old things are passed away; behold all things are become new. — 2 Corinthians 5.17*

PRAYER: *Thank You, Lord, for Your mercy and transforming power in Rob's life. Please keep working, cleansing and changing my life, too, for Christ's glory. Amen.*

Paratrooper Chuck Dean in
Vietnam with the 173rd Airborne.

Chuck Dean today in Seattle.
ACW Press staff, author, and
counselor.

Twenty-Six

MAKING PEACE WITH MY PAST

Chuck Dean's Story

God takes life's broken pieces and gives us unbroken peace.
— W.D. Gough

In February of 1963, about the time the Beatles were making their first appearance on the Ed Sullivan show, I stood staring at a life-size poster cutout in the window of a US Army recruiting office. As I gazed at the large photo of a tall, clean-shaven, rugged soldier, I could see myself in that same uniform. It was his spit-shined jump boots that led me to sign up to be a paratrooper. I was gung-ho and I wanted to go to war, win some medals, and come home as a respected man who had served his country in an elite forces unit.

After my jump training I was assigned to the 82nd Airborne Division. I re-enlisted to leave the 82nd and to be re-assigned to the 173rd Airborne in Okinawa. Then I spent the next year jungle training on Okinawa and Taiwan.

In May of 1965, President Johnson ordered my unit into South Vietnam. We were the first regular Army combat unit to enter the war. We thought we could win a few medals and get back safe and sound in a matter of weeks. But it didn't work that way. After one year in Vietnam it was time to return to the US.

At last we were coming home in one piece. We had turned in our weapons and were confined to a tiny barbed-wire compound on Ton Sanh Nhut Air Base. After dozens of cans of beer, we scrounged for a place to sleep. Our plane would be arriving in four hours. Our duty was over...we were going back to the "world." Everything would be right again.

I managed to find a mattress inside a corrugated tin shack. Just before falling into a drunken dream I was rattled to the bone by the concussion of mortar explosions. Instinctively, I threw the mattress over me as air-bursting mortar rounds ripped through the air. I pounded my fists into the ground, "You're not going to get me, Charlie!" Then I broke and cried out to God, "Oh God, I've been through too much to be taken out now."

As suddenly as it had begun, the explosions ceased. My thoughts of God vanished in the confusion. I heard the wounded crying out. Seven teenage soldiers, with their tours complete, died that morning. After spending a year in hell, this was their reward. *They, the ones who died that night, were the lucky ones...they escaped every memory and hidden side effect of Vietnam...we did not.*

Eighteen hours from that compound of death, I found myself in San Francisco International Airport. These people whom I had spent two years dreaming of coming back to, were all like foreigners to me. I felt myself beginning to lose my bearings and a deep confusion set in.

After being discharged, I found work and tried to live a normal civilian life in Seattle. The trauma of Vietnam was too much and a debilitating depression set in. I soon discovered that the only time I could put up with other people was when I was dead drunk. When that didn't work, I isolated myself and smoked pot until I became unconscious.

Three months later I entered another Army recruiting station to sign up for another hitch. Upon my return to active duty I was assigned to Drill Instructor School. The next two years I trained thousands of new soldiers, preparing them for Vietnam. My life was a maze of depression-ridden conflicts, doubts and further alienation. Every recruit was going to 'Nam, and it was my job, in eight weeks, to cut his hair off and convince him to pull the trigger on someone ten thousand miles from home.

My difficulties with work and relationships persisted. I married. We had a good friendship but getting close was difficult and we had more than our share of problems.

I came up for discharge again. It was at this point that I began to search to discover my spirituality. I had a feeling that my problems from Vietnam were not just psychological...it had to have some spiritual meaning.

To escape the emptiness and pain I, with my wife, immersed myself in the New Age movement and occult. It was one mystical teaching after another, and things went from bad to worse. My wife and I divorced. I bought a typewriter and began to purge myself of Vietnam ghosts by writing a long journal. I lived on beer and chicken, and wrote until I passed out from the alcohol each day. Thus began my writing career.

I became obsessed with trying to right every wrong I could find with the government structure through a militia organization. Soon I was under investigation by the FBI. It was at this point that my stress, insomnia and depression got the best of me. I broke down and called another paratrooper. I called and simply said, "Bill, I need a friend right now." He replied, "Chuck, you need the Lord." This surprised me. A week earlier I may have laughed, but at this particular moment, my life was in shambles. I was at the point of need that God had waited a long time for. Like a lifeguard waiting until a drowning man stops flailing the water so he can save him, Jesus stood by and waited for me to stop trying to survive by my own means and give up and rely solely upon Him. It was time for this soldier to surrender.

I brushed away tears I had not shed in almost twenty years and heard myself say, "Yeah, that's one thing I haven't tried...maybe that's what I need to do."

Then my friend said, "Are you willing to pray with me about it?" I agreed to because I knew my life needed an overhaul and I was out of answers. I also knew that if I kept trying "my" ways it meant certain disaster and more grief for everyone. That afternoon, on the phone, I prayed with Bill and gave my heart, soul and life to the Lord Jesus Christ.

When I got off the phone, I felt different. There was a peace in my mind that I hadn't felt before, a sense of release far beyond any drug or "method" I had ever tried before.

As time went on the heavy symptoms of Post Traumatic Stress Disorder (PTSD) felt like another part of life that I had once lived. The nightmares and horrible mental images that hounded me for all those years were diminishing day by day. It was as if Jesus was taking all of these troubled mental pictures from my subconscious mind and mounting them in a photo album. I could see them from time to time, but they no longer contained the same power over me they once had.

SCRIPTURE: *Peace I leave with you, My peace I give unto you: not as the world gives, give I unto you. Let not your heart be troubled, neither let it be afraid. — John 14.27*

PRAYER: *Thank You, Father, for your heart peace that passes all human understanding. May I rest in Your supernatural promise no matter what this day brings forth. In Jesus' matchless name. Amen.*

Lt. Jim Horsley, US Navy, fighter pilot and Blue Angel

Jim Horsley, today in Seattle

★ Twenty-Seven ★

THE BLUE ANGEL

by Jim Horsley

If we lose the war in the air, we lose the war, and we lose it quickly.
    —Field Marshall Viscount Montgomery of Alamein (1882-1976)

On Monday morning 10 April 1972, the USS *Midway* steamed out of San Francisco Bay, bound for the Vietnam war zone.

Neither Mike Penn nor Gary Shank (both A-7 pilots), nor myself, knew what was in store. Mike would spend seven months in a North Vietnam prisoner of war (POW) camp before being released. Gary would be killed in action. And I would come home, grateful to still be alive, yet not knowing I'd been wounded, although in a different way.

Bob Ponton, my bombardier/navigator (B/N), and I had been flying together as a crew since our A-6 training on Whidbey Island. Now, working together, we had to plan for every contingency. His role in the cockpit was to operate the navigation, radar and weapons systems. Mine was to ensure we had an equal number of takeoffs and landings. I had to get our jet in position to drop its weapons load and return safely from the target area. Bob was a skilled B/N, with a gentle demeanor but a bulldog resolve. I had great respect for his ability and character, and I couldn't have asked for a better partner in the air.

On 29 April, the day we launched to An Loc, the ship was steaming toward Vietnam, still some five hundred miles off the coast. We were so far out that most of the launch aircraft required in-flight refueling just to make it to the target and back to the ship. The primary incentive, of course, was to fly successful missions. A "bonus" was the additional sixty-five dollars of combat pay everyone on the *Midway* received for each month in combat. Some bonus. We would find out soon enough that the extra pay would pencil out to about a buck-sixty per mission. How was I going to spend all that extra cash?

"A-6s holding high, descend to one zero thousand and report visual on me, over."

As we leveled off, the FAC's radio crackled. "Intruders, the area is hot with enemy presence in all sectors. Civilians have abandoned the area. Your target is two tanks parked right in the middle of town that's been vacated. Notify when visual on the target, over."

Each pilot rapidly scanned the maze of buildings and identified the tanks. Calling, "Tally Ho, XO." The XO then made a similar call to the FAC, who immediately replied, "Give me four bombs each on three passes, you're cleared in hot."

I adjusted my flight path to establish some separation from the other two bombers. Seconds later, Presley's A-6 pitched slightly nose high, then abruptly rolled 135 degrees to the left then down, as he simultaneously called, "Lead's in hot." Moments later, on a dive path offset to his right, I replicated the same roll-in.

The war was on.

I rolled back to wings level at 40 degrees nose down. With my jet accelerating to 480 knots, two olive-green enemy tanks snuggled against a large building filled up the bombsight mounted on top of my instrument panel.

Everything I had trained for in Pensacola, Corpus Christi, Meridian, and Whidbey Island coalesced in this one moment. As Bob called out our altitudes at one-thousand-foot increments during the dive, I adjusted the control stick. Then, as we passed through forty-five hundred feet, without changing my grip, my right thumb depressed the small red "pickle" button on top of the stick grip. Four bombs rippled off the aircraft. Quickly, I pulled the stick back in my lap to get the nose up and away from the target area. Pressed back in my seat by the force of five g's, I snapped the plane hard right to foil any anti-aircraft gunners below.

"Great pass, great pass! Bombs on target!" the FAC called on the radio. I was barely back on level flight path when the FAC said, "Additional tanks are now moving down the street. See the building with the thatched roof next to the palm trees?"

"Roger, that," I said. And down we went. Again.

Several hours after landing, I walked into the ship's ready room and read the afternoon's results: "Flight of Intruders, lead aircraft November Fox Five Zero Two on target at fourteen hundred. Three tanks destroyed, one damaged." Launch, strike, land, and debrief. Then rest up for the next flight. I was ready to go out and earn another dollar and sixty cents.

UNDERNEATH MY VISOR

As the war crept toward a slow, tiresome pullout of American forces, Vietnam attached itself to my memory bank:

• The night sky in Haiphong Harbor awash with green and white tracers aimed at the A-6 that Bob Ponton and I brought screaming in only two hundred feet over the water. Bob shrieks himself hoarse telling me to "Take it up! Take it up!" because without higher altitude, his radar won't find our target. Once I tell him to look outside, Bob pulls his head up from his navigator's screen, takes one look at the lethal green shower exploding directly out his window and then, in a moment of unscripted hilarity, betrays his navigator bias and yells, "Take it down! Take it down!"

- The sound of many twenty-one gun salutes provided during our regular hangar deck memorial services for fellow aviators who hadn't returned.
- A drawer full of combat action awards that seemed meaningless in the context of the cost.
- A lifetime of midnight hamburgers and tasteless Kool-Aid.
- A photo of our squadron, including Mike Bixel, my roommate, whose aircraft's landing gear sheared off on a rainy nighttime landing, forcing him to eject as his burning jet slid down the flight deck, igniting an inferno. He, along with four others, died instantly. He was my roommate, my friend. Crewcut. Nice smile. Always steady, always there. Until that night.

In January 1973, we could see the end coming in Vietnam. With only a few weeks left before our country ceased its military involvement in the war, Mike McCormick and Arlo Clark launched on a night strike against a heavily defended weapons facility northwest of Vinh.

They never came back.

Officially, they would be listed as "Missing in Action." When I heard the news, I insisted on flying the initial search-and-rescue flight. Just prior to dawn, two hours after they had failed to return from their ill-fated mission, I was airborne for their target area. I streaked deep into the thick cloud cover that obscured their intended flight route, oblivious to the threat of enemy weapons.

I picked up no radio signal from their emergency beacon or radios.

I found no trace of their aircraft.

For a moment in the cockpit, I was sitting again at Jackie Jensen's Restaurant in Oakland with Sonya, Arlo, and his wife, Tonya. We were smiling and laughing two days before heading into a war we barely understood.

Somewhere over North Vietnam, I stared straight ahead. Behind the dark helmet visor that shielded my face, I felt the tears pour down my cheeks. I couldn't stop them. For once, I didn't want to. I wept for Arlo and for Mike. I wept with bitterness over the death of two close friends and the senseless war I had somehow managed to survive.

How had I made it through?

The best I could come up with was that I had been, and still was, an ordinary individual who had been thrown into some extraordinary circumstances and that I had come out the other side feeling a sense of accomplishment—and sadness. I was now a more resilient, more self-determined man, not yet fully aware of what I had gained. And lost.

We returned to our home base at the Naval Air Station on Whidbey Island on a cold, gray afternoon, 2 March 1973, eleven months, over two hundred missions and three hundred day and night carrier landings after leaving for Vietnam. Welcomed by the drums and bugles of a patriotic band and a bucket of champagne, I climbed out of my A-6 and renewed the reality of what things awaited—a wife who loved me, a daughter who captured my attention, and a son who grabbed me by the neck.

That afternoon, we commemorated our return and our losses by thundering over the base in a missing-man formation. I returned from Vietnam as a proven warrior who had been successful beyond my wildest dreams. And I was still oblivious to how much higher I would climb, with my visor firmly in place.

Seattle's Lake Washington shimmered in the August afternoon sun. It was the last day of Seafair, capped by the traditional Blue Angels airshow, and half a million spectators were thrilled by our demonstration. As was I...wing tips dancing softly only three feet from my helmet as we gracefully performed our maneuvers at astonishingly low altitudes and thundering airspeeds.

Later that afternoon at a festive lakeside VIP reception, I basked in the status and acclaim of being one of the "best of the best." And though I reveled in the adulation, life on the inside was becoming frayed and fragile. I couldn't define it at the time, but the signs of a greater reality were about to become unmistakable.

As evening approached, the champagne bottles were dry, the hors d' oeuvres were gone, and I was walking down the hall at the city's Edgewater Hotel. I opened my door, stepped into the darkness, and stretched out on the carpet, utterly depleted and emotionally exhausted.

Why, after I had accomplished so much—flown so far, so high, so fast—did I feel such a deep inner emptiness? I blamed it on the intensity of our schedule and a pending career change, and the next morning as we left for yet another city, I pulled the gold visor on my helmet down on my questions, added power, and left them behind.

Two years later, in the midst of my growing commercial real estate development career, those earlier questions still lingered. Only the landscape had changed. We were living in Lake Oswego, Oregon. Sonya began attending church with the kids in an attempt to hold our family together. Reluctantly, I followed, mostly so I wouldn't be noticed by my absence. One Sunday a month later, contrary to my "instructions," she filled out a guest registration card. It wasn't long before I received a call inviting me to our church men's retreat on the Oregon Coast. It was a short conversation because it doesn't take much time to say no.

While I was reluctant to engage the church, I found myself leaning forward on Sundays as the pastor told stories of authentic people whose lives had been changed by a relevant God. The biblical perspectives he shared, wrapped in the personal warmth and integrity with which he spoke, began to touch me in places of real need. My interest in faith began to grow, but I wasn't about to trap myself at a retreat with a bunch of men I didn't know, in a setting where I wasn't in control.

A few days later I left for an overnight business trip to our headquarters in California. Following a late dinner and an exhausted return to my hotel, restless and disturbed, I couldn't escape the growing disconnect I felt between my public persona and my private struggle. I wasn't nearly as in control as I wanted others to believe, and the Edgewater Hotel feelings returned.

When I arrived home, I phoned the church and asked if it was too late to sign up for the retreat. It wasn't, and two weeks later I squeezed into the last remaining car, right next to the pastor. Once settled into the conference center, I didn't say much to the other men. However, from their first "hellos" they accepted me, no questions asked. I didn't feel judged or ignored. I felt welcomed and affirmed.

That Saturday afternoon I walked on the beach, alone, as alone as I had ever been. I thought about where I'd been and who I was. I pondered the selfishness and hardness that had crowded into my existence. I hadn't been that way in the six years of Sunday school as a child. I hadn't behaved that way in Young Life. I wasn't the same man that Sonya thought she'd married as a bright-eyed college student.

On the beach, I began to understand why. My pursuit of attention and acceptance had seduced my soul, and my yearning for recognition was a futile attempt to ignore the shame that came from not living a greater truth and purpose. The sporadic attendance at Christmas and Easter services seemed hollow and hypocritical. At what point had I sacrificed all that had meaning and chosen a path that had fed the lie?

When I got back to my room and sat on the bed, tears of regret flooded down my cheeks.

At the session that night, a number of men stood up and talked about the reality of God in their lives. I sat and listened. All I could hear was the truth of my failure in the things that should have mattered.

I couldn't stonewall this any more.

I had gained elite status with the Blues. I had become one of the best in the world at what I wanted to be, and experienced a victory without substance. The Jesus in my Bible achieved no status, yet had claimed the ultimate victory.

I decided that either Christ was going to be real in my life or He was not. Late that night in the darkness of my room, I admitted my fears and failures, and prayed for a relationship with Christ. He answered. And I immediately experienced an overwhelming sense of His presence, forgiveness, acceptance and love.

The next night over dinner at home I raised my protective visor just a crack and told Sonya about the change. "I'm not sure what this is all means, but over the weekend I made a firm decision that I've got to be serious about my relationship with Christ, and His promise of a new beginning. I don't know where it will lead, but life has to offer more than it has in the past."

And by God's grace it has. Beyond any airshow or personal accomplishment or combat experience, the fulfillment, fruitfulness and fullness of my life in faith has offered more than I could have ever imagined.

—Condensed with permission from *"A Different Kind of Courage"*
by Jim Horsley, with Mark Cutshall
Word Publishing; ISBN 0-8499-4015-X Hard cover

SCRIPTURE: *My son, if you will receive My Words and hide my commandments with you, so that you incline your ear unto wisdom and apply your heart to understanding…if you seek her as silver and search for her as for hid treasures; then you shall understand the fear of the Lord and find the Knowledge of God. — Proverbs 2.1,2,4,5*

PRAYER: *Lord, give me the courage to raise the visor of my life to you. Help me to look within my heart to see the real condition. Help me to understand the fear of the Lord. Amen.*

⋆ **VII** ⋆

Commitment

The squares of Europe are littered with the statues of generals, admirals and statesmen whose titles and deeds we have forgotten. But still alive in memory are the men and women who attempted more than they could carry out and left unfinished work that their successors completed.

— Alec Waugh

D. Enright

Twenty-Eight

THE GIFT

by Bob Boardman

Is there any greater gift that we can give than the sacrifice of our own selves? Churchill said, "We make a living by what we get, but we make a life by what we give."

It was Christmas season in the big city of Brooklyn, New York with all of its festive mood, busy shoppers and attendant joy. Throughout, families were anticipating the return of loved ones, the traditional holiday meals and the happy exchange of what people hoped would be the perfect gift. Yuletide decorations festooned stores, streets, apartments and homes.

Yet in the midst of all this celebration, here or there the tide of human tragedy and heartache could not be held at bay. The cycles of life and death held to their grim course. This was illustrated in a story I read in the *Readers Digest* many years ago about the father of a Marine.

An elderly man suddenly collapsed as he was walking in downtown Brooklyn. Fellow pedestrians came to his rescue, quickly calling an ambulance, which rushed him to King's County Hospital.

In the emergency ward the stricken man slowly regained consciousness and weakly began to call for his son. The attending nurse learned that his son was a Marine stationed at Camp Lejeune, North Carolina. There were no other relatives.

As rapidly as possible, the Red Cross traced his son. A Marine officer in a jeep finally found him on maneuvers in the field. He was rushed to the airport in time to catch the one last flight that might enable him to reach his dying father in time. It was evening, just after dark when the young Marine reached the hospital.

When he entered the dimly lit hospital room, the attending nurse kept repeating to the father, "Your son is here." At first it seemed that because of the heavy sedation the father might not be able to respond. Then slowly and weakly he reached out his workworn hand.

The Marine grabbed his hand and wrapped his tough fingers around the limp grip. Throughout the night he squeezed messages of love and encouragement.

Nights are long in hospitals, but the Marine sat there holding the old man's hand, offering words of hope and strength along with prayers for God's will to prevail. Occasionally the nurse suggested that he move away and rest awhile. He refused.

The dying man, unable to speak, only held his son's hand. Toward dawn his grip slowly loosened and in a few moments his soul departed from his body and slipped out into eternity.

The Marine bowed his head and, still holding the warm hand of the once vibrant, hard-working father, reverently said his final prayer. Then he slowly, gently placed the limp hand across the now lifeless chest.

He then notified the nurse. As she came into the room she started to offer words of sympathy.

The Marine turned and said, "Who was that man?"

The nurse stammered, "Why, he was your father."

"No, he wasn't. I never saw him before in my life."

The nurse, with continuing amazement said, "Why then didn't you say something when I took you to him?"

"I knew right off that there had been a mistake. But I also knew that he needed his son and his son just wasn't here. When I realized he was too sick to tell whether or not I was his son, I figured he really needed me. So I stayed."

Two days later a message arrived from the Red Cross saying that they had located the real son. He was on his way from Camp Lejeune and would arrive soon to make funeral arrangements.

The two men had the same names, similar serial numbers and both were from New York. The wrong Marine became the right son at the right time, showing there are still people who care. In a sometimes cruel, callous and uncaring world there are still those who will pay a price to bring hope and encouragement to the helpless.

This young Marine offered a dying man *the priceless gift* of comfort, hope and the sacrifice of his own personal schedule and convenience. This kind of gift cannot be purchased at any price in any store. It is, indeed, a rare treasure today.

The noble deed of this young Leatherneck is a vivid reminder of God's amazing gift to us two thousand years ago. We are so much like the helpless, dying man in King's County Hospital. Our penchant for wrongdoing and wrong choices over a lifetime should bring us to a place of complete dependence upon the Living God, the One who created us.

His *indescribable gift* to us in our helpless and spiritually dead condition is that of hope and eternal life through Jesus Christ His beloved Son. The Savior voluntarily left the comfort and glory of heaven to die in our place on the Cross. He was then raised from the dead to give us hope beyond the grave. He sits beside us waiting for our response.

If you have not yet received *God's matchless gift*, will you not do that today? He awaits your outstretched hand and upturned heart.

★   ★   ★

SCRIPTURE: *Thanks be to God for His indescribable Gift [of Jesus Christ]. — 2 Corinthians 9.15*

PRAYER: *Lord, give me the same spirit of generosity that You had when You gave Jesus Christ as a gift for my salvation. Amen.*

* Twenty-Nine *

KUNISHI RIDGE, OKINAWA

by Bob Boardman

*Death in combat is not the end of the fight but its peak, and
since combat is a part, and at times the sum total of life,
death which is the peak of combat, is not the destruction of
life, but its fullest, most powerful expression.*

— General Moshe Dayan, 1971

On 17 June 2002, fifty-seven years to the hour and the day when
the battle of Kunishi Ridge ended for our decimated tank platoon, I stood on the reverse slope of the ridge. Anti-tank and
Japanese rifle fire had ended the battle and several lives in 1945. We
who were wounded and survived will never forget Kunishi.

Now in 2002 so many vivid memories coursed through my heart and my head regarding the "Father's Day Massacre." It was my privilege to lead a group of thirty-five people, mostly Americans and a couple of Okinawan friends in a memorial service for the 1,150 Marine casualties, wounded and killed on Kunishi Ridge.

I've never told parts of this story before, not even to my closest loved ones. Should I try? I'm not sure I can tell it right. To me, Kunishi is a sacred place of amazing, almost unprecedented human sacrifice.

Those eight days seemed like an eternity, fighting against this well-defended ridge of jagged escarpments, coral ravines, natural and man-made caves, and Okinawan concrete burial vaults converted into pillboxes on southern Okinawa.

Out of my three campaigns in C Company First Tank Battalion, First Marine Division, it seems that Kunishi Ridge has been burned indelibly, not just into my conscious mind only, but also into my innermost heart and being. Even as I pen these feeble words I weep.

The US Tenth Army, made up of four Army and three Marine divisions, landed on Okinawa 1 April 1945. The battle for Kunishi Ridge and its adjoining environs, weeks later, was the last organized major ridge of resistance before the island was officially declared secure on 21 June, almost three months after the landing.

By the time we of the First Marine Division captured the major fishing village of Itoman in southern Okinawa, we were now face-to-face with Kunishi, separated by an ominous valley a thousand yards across. All defending Japanese troops and hundreds of Americans would breathe their last in the valley and on that rugged ridge of destruction and death.

Amazingly, on 31 May, LtGen. Simon Bolivar Buckner, commander of the US Tenth Army, declared to his staff, "It's all over now, but cleaning up pockets of resistance." Ironically, eighteen days later, the last day of the battle for Kunishi and Mezado Ridges, the general was killed. He got too close to "the cleanup," against the advice of his staff.

This is "the battlefield way" that no man can truly predict or comprehend—only God. Many believe General Buckner was slated to command the Allied force destined to invade mainland Japan in November 1945.

Casualties in all units of the Tenth Army, both Army and Marines, were extremely heavy in two and a half months of sustained fighting prior to the battle of Kunishi Ridge.

The 2nd Battalion, 1st Marine Regiment, 1st Marine Division, landed on Okinawa on 1 April with 939 men and received 608 replacements during the campaign. Of this combined total of 1,547, the battalion suffered 902 killed or wounded, and they had to evacuate another 567 for sickness, including "combat fatigue" cases. Ninety-five percent of all the officers and men who served in this battalion were either killed or evacuated at one point during the fighting on Okinawa.

— Leatherneck, November. 1997

Twelve thousand relatively fresh troops of the Japanese Twenty-Fourth Division plus assorted survivors of other enemy units defended Kunishi. All approaches were completely covered with interlocking fields of fire. The Japanese Fukkaku defense system had interfaced Okinawa's ridges, escarpments and hills with sixty miles of laboriously hand-dug caves and tunnels, not employing one stick of explosives.

So well-sited were the Japanese guns in the caves of Kunishi that a Marine could not advance a single step in daylight across the line of departure without getting drilled by high-velocity fire.

— Ibid, Leatherneck

In the First Marine Division, casualties were especially high among veteran tactical leadership—company commanders, platoon sergeants and lieutenants.

Because of the shortage of leaders, the Seventh Marine Regimental commander, Col. Edward Snedeker, ordered Fox and George Companies to lead an innovative night assault against Kunishi. Their orders were, "The ridge is to be gained with grenades and bayonets. No packs. Ponchos looped in back belt. Rations in pockets. Two canteens of water. Minimum of four grenades." This bold and daring initiative seized a three-hundred-yard pocket on Kunishi's crest.

Reinforcing these two companies on the ridge became a major challenge. Moving across the thousand-yard no-man's valley to assault the enemy meant mounting casualties from the enemies machine-gun, rifle, mortar and 47mm and 76mm anti-tank fire. Tanks were the answer.

> *Col. Snedeker and his battalion commanders soon realized drastic measures were in order to relieve the pressure on Kunishi Ridge. The infantry commanders turned to the tankers for solutions. The C Company Tank Company Commanding Officer, Jerry Jerue, his platoon leaders (Charley Nelson, Jerry Atkinson and Tom Duddleson) and several of the tank commanders, devised a plan to employ tanks in a ferry system to haul the infantry up to the ridge. Col. Snedeker and Col. "Jeb" Stuart quickly approved this unorthodox idea.*
>
> — Col. Walter MuMu Moore,
> then Executive Officer of C Company, First Tank Battalion

A scene I've lived with for fifty-seven years of my life and have never shared with anyone, to my knowledge, involved a gravely wounded Marine from the Seventh Marine Regiment. Our tanks from the First Tank Battalion on Kunishi had a total of twenty-two knocked out by enemy fire. I was the driver of two of those tanks. Two days before 17 June, my tank was disabled on the front slope of Kunishi. Besides engaging the enemy in deadly firefights, our tanks served in the following unique ways.

Five hundred fifty combat troops and ninety tons of ammo, food and water were delivered through that deadly valley and up onto the ridge by our thirty-ton Shermans. We also evacuated over six hundred wounded off of the ridge—we put the walking wounded inside the tanks and the seriously wounded lay on the outside. Certain gravely wounded Marines could not be placed inside our tanks, but on the exposed back. Sometimes a tank crewman took upon himself to ride on the back to keep the injured Marine from rolling off and to give some small measure of help and comfort.

Our C Company made several trips daily throughout that no-quarter, eight-day battle. One day I was on the back taking care of a badly wounded infantryman. At this stage of the battle there were no stretchers available.

I talked to this young, fair-haired teenager over the roar of the twin diesel engines right beneath us. I held him firmly as our Sherman slowly crept down the crude, narrow, rocky coral road that we hoped would get us through No-Man's Valley and to the battalion aid station set up in an Okinawan hut in the village of Itoman.

I learned his name which I've long since forgotten. He looked like young Mr. mid-America. At first I couldn't spot his wound, but noticed his eyes were glazing over, indicating he was mercifully going into shock.

Then as I more carefully looked down his body I spotted his unbandaged wound. To my own shock I saw that where his private parts once were was now just a bloody pulp. This is the place on the body where every fighting man hopes and prays, consciously or subconsciously, that he will never be hit.

This young comrade, perhaps a new replacement into his unit, was mercifully dying. Those that carried him off the killing field no doubt knew that and gave more attention to those who had a better chance to live. In our war we didn't have protective flak jackets.

Above the din of the roaring engines I recited the Twenty-Third or Marine's Psalm. The young lad assured me of his eternal destiny with the Lord and then I prayed for him. Months later I read his name in the KIA (Killed in Action) list in the Old Breed history.

Three or four days later the following comrades from C Company would join me in becoming casualties, adding to and making the 1,150 total casualties on our sector of Kunishi: Jerry Atkinson, Joe Alvarez, Robert Bennett, Bud Brenkert, Scuddly Hoffman, K.C. Smith. I salute each of these spirited, courageous comrades!

There is no surviving record of the extent of Japanese losses [on Kunishi], but they must have been considerable. The First Marine Division's "processing" of fortified positions was slow but memorable. White phosphorous, napalm and satchel charges, systematically applied, had a certain finality.

On August 29, well after Imperial Japan's [national] surrender, Col. Kikuji Hongo led 450 survivors of his 32nd Infantry Regiment out of Kunishi's cover to give themselves up to a US Army PsyWar team. The hollowed-out mile-long ridge had proven one hell of a fortress.

— Leatherneck, November 1997, pg. 35

I must make one thing very clear. I was no hero—I was just a twenty-one-year-old Marine trying to do his duty, often with fear and trembling. The real heroes were those infantrymen and corpsmen up on Kunishi Ridge who stayed there and tangled with the merciless enemy day and night.

For 1,150 of them, the only way off the ridge was to be carried off as WIA or KIA. At the conclusion of those eight days at Kunishi, these weary, bedraggled, war-worn warriors in their teens and early twenties, achieved the final victory. I shall never forget them and will hail them until the day I die. They purchased, with their precious blood, our freedom today.

SCRIPTURE: The Twenty-Third or Marine's Psalm: *The Lord is my shepherd; I shall not want. He makes me to lie down in green pastures; He leads me beside the still waters. He restores my soul; He leads me in the paths of righteousness for His name's sake. Yea, though I walk through the valley of the shadow of death, I will fear no evil; for You are with me; Your rod and Your staff, they comfort me. You prepare a table before me in the presence of my enemies; You anoint my head with oil; my cup runs over. Surely goodness and mercy shall follow me all the days of my life; and I will dwell in the house of the Lord forever.*

PRAYER: *Please pray over the above Twenty-third Psalm phrase by phrase, making it your prayer.*

Pvt. Bud Brenkert, USMCR, in Ballarat, Australia, 1943

Thirty

BUD BRENKERT'S MOST HEROIC ACT

by Bob Boardman

IN MEMORIAM • 1922-1999

Daily, difficult choices in our marriage and in our lives equal or surpass battlefield heroics.

An unanticipated phone call came late at night from Joanie, Bud Brenkert's youngest daughter, saying that Bud was in a coma from mesenteric ischemia, a fatal disease. It kills the bowels and sends toxic poison into the bloodstream, resulting in septic shock. One day Bud, 77, a retired GMC lawyer, was golfing; the next day, after abdominal agony, he was fighting a losing battle for his life.

My wife, Jean, and I left the next morning on an already planned trip. My stay in Philadelphia at the First Marine Division reunion was cut short by a phone call from Joanie, Bud's youngest daughter, that said Bud was dying and "could you come?" The three daughters felt Bud was holding on until I got there.

Cornelius "Bud" Brenkert and I were in Marine boot camp in San Diego at the same time in late 1942, though in different platoons. One of his earliest memories of me was when I outboxed a Canadian weightlifter.

Bud, a hefty, handsome Dutchman from Detroit, was built like a heavyweight himself with massive chest and shoulders but he was not very nimble on his feet. Along with several hundred other graduates from the accelerated seven week wartime boot camp, we ended up in Infantry Training at Camp Elliot.

One day the Corps announced that they needed tankers. So they put into operation their scientific selection system (SSS). "All A's, B's, C's and D's fall in on the right. You are now tankers!"

Alvarez, Bahde, Barwick, Boardman, Brenkert, Christensen, etc.—all together we went through tank training at Jaques Farm in San Diego, then into the Seventeenth Replacement Battalion. Eventually we sailed on a twenty-eight-day adventure cruise to Melbourne, Australia.

There we were integrated into C Company First Tank Battalion, First Marine Division, of Guadalcanal fame. Two years and three campaigns later we motley privates had become sergeants, corporals, tank commanders, gunners and drivers.

On 17 June 1945 in an Okinawan sugar cane field, we faced the supreme challenge of our young lives as we were involved in the "Father's Day Massacre," just over Kunishi Ridge.

Seriously wounded, I ended up on a stretcher on the back of Bud Brenkert's and Old Man Christensen's tank. As we traveled through a no-man's valley that held Japanese snipers, Bud left the protection of his armored turret and lay his body across mine to shield me. He steadfastly refused my feeble hand gesture to get back inside the tank.

For this and other selfless acts of heroism, Bud was awarded the Silver Star, and also a Purple Heart.

Now in a Detroit hospital I was privileged to spend the last six hours of Bud's life at his bedside with his beautiful, loving daughters,

Barbara, Susan and Joanie. No dying man had such tender, tearful care. The four of us deeply believed that Bud could hear us, even in his coma, as we talked to and prayed for him.

Then the girls left the room so that I could talk to Bud alone. I shared Psalm 23, the Marines' psalm, prayed, told Bud he need not fear in his journey through the Valley of the Shadow of Death, if his trust and hand held tightly to Jesus Christ, His death and resurrection. I shared names of old C Company buddies and assured him of their heart concerns and prayers.

For the first time in two weeks of his comatose state, Bud opened his eyes for about two or three minutes and slowly blinked several times, just as the girls reentered the room. The four of us and a nurse all gave praise to God as we witnessed a true miracle of Bud being able to look around. Within about four hours Bud took the journey of no return.

In the fifty-six years I had known Bud, he was not an outwardly religious man. But his family and I believe he had a premonition about his pending death and may have prepared his eternal soul to meet God and the judgment that follows. Two months previously he had bought two grave plots. When he filled out the papers he requested that I conduct his funeral. He also chose three hymns: "The Old Rugged Cross," "Onward Christian Soldiers" and "Amazing Grace." He asked to be buried in his Marine uniform.

Bud Brenkert, like Private Ryan in the recent movie, a "good man," performed several heroic acts on the battlefields of the Pacific, including helping to save my life. But I'm not sure the battlefield was the apex of his heroism.

You see, Bud's beloved wife, Cathy, a godly, wonderful woman, has had progressive Alzheimer's for the last eight years. Bud steadfastly, personally took care of Cathy, refusing to place her in a nursing home. This took its toll on our old comrade. I can't help but think that this selfless deed of commitment to Cathy was his most heroic act. Semper Fi and farewell, Buddy!

SCRIPTURE: *For when we were still helpless, Christ at the proper time died for us, ungodly men. Now a man will scarcely ever give his life for an upright person, though once in awhile, a man is brave enough to die for a good friend. But God proves His love for us by the fact that Christ died for us while we were still sinners. — Romans 5.6,7,8*

PRAYER: *Lord of the heart, will You not now day by day lay the spiritual foundation in my unworthy life, so that when the crisis comes, I will be willing to sacrifice for others. In Jesus' name. Amen.*

☆   ☆   ☆

CITATION

The President of the United States takes pleasure in presenting the SILVER STAR MEDAL to SERGEANT CORNELIUS BRENKERT, UNITED STATES MARINE CORPS RESERVE, for service as set forth in the following CITATION:

For conspicuous gallantry and intrepidity while serving as a Tank Commander of Company C, First Tank Battalion, First Marine Division, in action against enemy Japanese forces on Okinawa, Ryukyu Island, 17 June 1945. When his tank was hit four times and several of his crew members were seriously wounded by fire from an enemy anti-tank gun during an assault well forward of the front lines, Sergeant Brenkert observed that the tank of his Platoon Leader was disabled and on fire and, skillfully maneuvering his vehicle alongside the burning tank despite continuing hostile antitank fire, effected the rescue of its crew members. His outstanding courage and devotion to duty were in keeping with the highest traditions of the United States Naval Service.

For the President, John L. Sullivan, Secretary of the Navy.

D. Enright

Thirty-One

A Salute to the Fallen

by Bob Boardman

*Death is the great adventure besides which moon landings
and space trips pale into insignificance.*

— J. Bayly

The endless stream of veterans and their spouses taking
the journey of no return from the eras of WWII,
Korea and Vietnam is turning from a steady, gentle stream
into a mounting flood-swollen torrent overflowing its banks.

This fact should not bring alarm, but rather a heart of
preparation and thanksgiving for a generation that under
the hand of God, helped bring world peace, stability and the
overthrow of absolute evil.

At the moment of penning these words, I think of the following friends, comrades and wives who recently have failed to emerge from the Valley of the Shadow of Death: Warren Myers, Mr. Shirley Laird, Carl Hodges, Denis O'Brien, Hugh Harris, Florence Seely, Elizabeth Jaunal, Dave Morken, Bill Gunner McMillian, Ray Gripman, and States Rights Jones. Yes, that is his true name.

You never have to wonder what this son of the deep South's parents thought of the authority of the federal government! States Rights, however, did faithfully serve his country as a career combat officer in the US Marine Corps. We sorely miss these and scores of others who have been taken from us.

There are many others of our number now in hospitals, infirm at home or in hospices who will very soon step out into the unknown void and join those already departed. The so-called Greatest Generation and those behind them are rapidly passing from the scene to join comrades from wartime who were suddenly and violently snatched away in the very prime of life.

The Department of Veterans Affairs predicts that "deaths among the G.I. Generation are likely to peak in 2008, when 620,000 veteran deaths are projected." These figures broken down, mean 51,666 deaths per month and over 1,700 veterans dying a day in 2008!

Every man must do two things alone; he must do his own believing and his own dying.

— Martin Luther

The above startling figure could pose the question—is it better to die young violently and suddenly in war, or is it best to live long and slowly die, withering away on the vine, gradually losing all physical and emotional facilities—yes, and even one's spiritual equilibrium, as I see happening now to a good friend of mine?

The Good Book in its incomparable wisdom tells us about the shortness of life compared to God's eternity. Summing up Psalm 90, it says that our life is like a flood that sweeps us away in a few dramatic moments; or like sleep and we forget all when awakened; or like grass that grows and is cut down; or like a story that is told and soon forgotten. The conclusion of the first twelve verses is this prayer of the Psalmist:

So teach us to number our days that we may apply our hearts unto wisdom. — Psalm 90.12

Our numbers dwindled rapidly and drastically during our respective wars. Now in a more peaceful era our ranks are again slowly ebbing. Nevertheless, the thinning of our ranks is dramatic.

John A Lejeune, legendary former Commandant of the Marine Corps, said this about the effect of battle and possible death in his memoirs:

There is no more powerful emotion known to man than that which permeates every fiber of his being when he goes into battle.

So it ought to be with us, the living, as we pay tribute to the fallen in war and in the present. We give thanks for their contributions to our nation, to the cause of freedom and justice internationally and to our own individual lives, and for their invaluable friendships.

Their deaths ought to permeate every fiber of our being and help prepare us for our own journey of no return. It should cause great heart-searching. Am I ready to meet my Maker, the Judge of everyone in heaven and in the earth, the Lord Jesus Christ?

The most momentous concern of man is the state he shall enter upon after this transitory life is ended.

— Clarke

As we salute the fallen, those who have gone before us, and as we consider our own mortality, may the following be our prayer as long as we draw our breath:

This God is our God for ever and ever. HE will be our guide even unto death. So we Your people and sheep of Your pasture will give You thanks forever: we will show forth Your praise to generation and generation. In Jesus' Name. Amen. — Psalm 48.14; 79.13

The basis for this prayer, to influence future generations, is surely a reason to live a long life, if it please God.

I personally want to leave a lasting legacy to the next generations and pray that God might see fit to fulfill this desire in my unworthy life.

☆ ☆ ☆

SCRIPTURE: *For David, after serving God's purpose in his own generation, died and was buried with his fathers...——- Acts 13.35*

PRAYER: *When it comes time to die, make sure all you have to do is die. Lord, help me to get ready today for that ultimate, final moment, whether in war or in peacetime! In Jesus' name, Amen.*

★ Acknowledgments ★

In 1992 and 1994, I had the privilege and challenge of running the New York City Marathon. The first time I was just turning sixty-eight and in 1994, I turned seventy. My second son, John, running with me, insisted on staying alongside all 26.2 miles, despite my urging him to go all out himself. We finished together in both races holding hands as we crossed the finish line in a blistering six hours plus.

I'll never forget those experiences and the encouragement John was to me by his enthusiastic words and his presence. Also the great city of New York won our hearts back then. The grueling marathon wound through each of the five boroughs.

All along the way spectators and bystanders cheered us along. We runners, thirty thousand strong, were mostly strangers from all over the US and around the world. Every so often there were little street bands and combos playing to let us know they were for us and that we should never give up.

My wife, Jean, along with John's wife, Yoko, pushing our grandson Preston in a stroller, hurried from one vantage point to another near the end. They cheered us on and gave moral support to us on that arduous course.

In the same way, I could not have completed the marathon labor of this book without the support of many Marines, loved ones and friends. Thank you. I am only able to name a few here:

★ General Anthony Zinni, US Marine Corps (Retired), a combat Marine with two tours in Vietnam and innumerable deployments through an illustrious career. The general has received awards from both the military and civilian worlds. I thank him for his willingness to, by faith, write the foreword.

★ Major General Jerry White, US Air Force Reserve (Retired), General Director of the Navigators and my leader for many years. A prolific writer and speaker, yet Jerry relates to the man on the street in a unique manner while he heads our mission of over four thousand staff worldwide.

* Colonel Walter Moore, US Marine Corps (Retired), veteran of three wars. Walt was the Executive Officer of C Company, First Tank Battalion in the battle of Okinawa. This salty warrior has been unceasing in urging me on and I thank him for composing the introduction and for his story in chapter 2.

* Chuck Dean of ACW Press, a former 173rd Army Airborne combat trooper in Vietnam. He and the staff of ACW have been very helpful, supportive and understanding of my purpose in this project. Chuck serves as national chaplain of the 173rd Airborne and is a prolific author. Also, many thanks to Fred Renich, General Manager, ACW press, and his staff for their diligent work on the book.

* Monte "Chuck" Unger, originally helped launch me into the writing world many years ago. He took a step away on this book, feeling I could do things more on my own. Nevertheless I sent all the manuscripts to Chuck for the final polish. He is an author, editor, a great counselor, Army veteran of Korea and committed to Marine Corps ideals of Honor, Courage and Commitment.

* Don Enright, award-winning wildlife artist, has captured the image of C-Rations being eaten by three warriors on the front cover following a hard-fought battle. In my mind, Don has "done it again," as with his cover painting for me in *Unforgettable Men in Unforgettable Times*. Don was a WWII US Navy B-24 nose gunner. He also did the pencil graphics.

* Ron "Sergeant" York (chapter 12) has kept my feet to the fire. Frequently we talk on the phone, and from Idaho, Ron would ask, "How's the book coming, Boardy?" Sometimes I didn't want to face the question, but I always needed to hear it! Especially at the twentieth mile of this marathon project and on toward the finish line when a runner-writer tends to "hit the wall."

* Arnie Lyshall, a member of the Puget Sound Chosin Few, gave me permission to use several of his splendid charcoal sketches of the First Marine Division in Korea. I have found great comradeship monthly with Arnie and other survivors of the harrowing battle of Korea and the Chosin Reservoir in the early 1950s.

* Dave Bishop, retired First Sergeant, USMC, police officer, author and avocado farmer in California. Dave and his wife Cathy have been constant in their example, encouragement and outreach to Marines.

* Jimmie Dean Coy, Colonel, US Army Reserve, the national surgeon of the Reserve Officer's Association. He is the medical consultant for the US Army Special Operations Command and the compiler and editor of *A Gathering of Eagles & Valor*. Jim has been a challenge and first class encourager of my writing efforts.

* Barbara Harmon, of Harmony Business Services, has done all of the typing and retyping of the manuscript. As can be imagined, this talented service is invaluable. I am deeply grateful.

* Janice Jantzen, Navigator senior secretary in many countries of the world, has in the last few weeks of organizing the final touches, helped me immeasurably, including important proofreading.

* My Family. My oldest, Holly, in New Bedford, MA; Laurel and Bob in Tacoma, WA; Paul and Judy in Seattle and also Heidi, my youngest in Seattle; John and Tonia in Tokyo have all been great cheerleaders. Our grandchildren, Ethan and Ashley, Heather and Matthew, Preston, Zoe and Cristian & our great-granddaughter, Arielle, all inspire me along the way.
Heidi, being in the same city, has assisted me in so many ways—her interest and enthusiasm, bookkeeping and updating addresses. Chuck Unger said to me, "Be sure that Heidi proofreads the manuscript. She is a whiz." Thanks, also, to Paul.

* My Beloved Wife Jean. It so happens that the publishing of *C-Rations for the Warrior's Heart* coincides with our fiftieth wedding anniversary on 1 August 2003. This lady is truly the light of my earthly life and my best friend and lover. I could not have accomplished this mountainous task without her wholehearted backing and invaluable input and proofreading.

* The combat veteran participants who wrote their stories or permitted me to write them and who make up the bulk of this tome. These are all personal friends except Frank Reasoner, in chapter 3, who was killed in action in Vietnam. I can attest to each of their courage, patriotism, and above-and-beyond-the-call-of-duty service to God and Country.

Great
Gift
Idea!

C-Rations for the Warrior's Heart
Order Form

(Copies can be signed. Please indicate clearly to whom you would like it signed.)

Postal orders: Bob Boardman
P.O. Box 25001
Seattle, WA 98165-1901

Author's E-mail: rrboardman@aol.com

Please send *C-Rations for the Warrior's Heart* to:

Name: _____

Address: _____

City: _____   State: _____

Zip: _____   Telephone: (_____) _____

Book Price: $14.99 (softcover)
$24.95 (hardcover)

Shipping: $2.95 for the first book and $1.00 for each additional book to
cover shipping and handling within US, Canada, and Mexico.
International orders add $6.00 for the first book and $2.00 for
each additional book.

Or order from:
ACW Press
85334 Lorane Hwy
Eugene, OR 97405

(800) 931-BOOK
(credit card)

or contact your local bookstore

A HIGHER HONOR

- Intriguing observations of Japanese honor and commitment in peacetime and war. Robert Boardman, wounded in a war of hate, returned to Japan, land of his former enemy, to live and minister for 33 years.

- Penetrating insights into the Japanese culture, philosophy and customs.

(Only available directly from the author).

$8 +$2.95 S&H

UNFORGETTABLE MEN IN UNFORGETTABLE TIMES

- No one can read this book and not be deeply touched by feelings of patriotism and the overwhelming presence of God and struggles for forgiveness and reconciliation that followed. Now in the fourth printing.

- Bob Boardman was a Marine who fought in three battles in the Pacific. He was personally decorated with the Silver Star and two Purple Hearts.

$13 + $2.95 S&H

- -

Name _____

Address _____

_____

Amount Enclosed $_____

Tel(_____)_____

(If you order both books, S&H is $2.95 total.)

Bob Boardman
PO Box 25001
Seattle, WA 98165-1901

For credit card orders on *Unforgettable Men* only, please call: (800) 917-BOOK